THE PATH OF LOVE

THE PATH

Meher Baba

OF LOVE

☿

SAMUEL
WEISER, INC.
NEW YORK

FIRST PUBLISHED 1976

© 1953, 1954, 1955, 1956, 1958, 1959, 1960, 1961, 1963,
1964, 1965, 1967, 1969 by The Universal Spiritual League
in America, Inc.
© 1976 by Adi K. Irani

SAMUEL WEISER, INC.
734 Broadway
New York, N.Y. 10003

Library of Congress Catalogue Card Number: 76–15540

ISBN 0-87728-309-5

Book design by
PERETZ KAMINSKY

Typography by
KENNETH R. PATTON
New York

Printed in the U.S.A. by
NOBLE OFFSET PRINTERS INC.

Meher Baba has said,

"I have come not to teach but to awaken."

Nevertheless, throughout the years, Meher Baba, the silent Avatar of the age, dictated on his alphabet board, and through his own unique *mudras* or hand gestures, a great deal of material about the various aspects of the Spiritual Path and its goal—God-Realization. Much of this material he gave to the *Awakener Magazine,* founded in 1953 to carry his message of love and truth to the West. It is this material which we have the privilege of reprinting here.

While reading it, one must bear in mind that Meher Baba's viewpoint is not that of an ordinary philosopher, thinker, or even advanced soul on the Path. His point of view is that of one who has *realized* the truth of God's Infinite Knowledge, Power and Bliss. I believe it is for this reason his words not only teach, but awaken. One can absorb them on the intellectual level and gain wisdom; one can be inspired by them on the intuitive level and get a taste of that *amrit* or divine bliss which the Shining Ones insist is our ultimate inheritance.

FILIS FREDERICK
Editor, *The Awakener Magazine*

October, 1975

A Short Biography of Meher Baba

Merwan Sheriar Irani, known as Meher Baba, was born in Poona, India, on February 25, 1894, of Persian parents. His father, Sheriar Irani, was of Zoroastrian faith and a true seeker of God. Merwan went to a Christian high school in Poona and later attended Deccan College. In 1913, while in college, a momentous event occurred in his life . . . the meeting with Hazrat Babajan, an ancient Mohammedan woman and one of the five Perfect Masters of the Age. Babajan gave him God-Realization and made him aware of his high spiritual destiny.

Eventually he was drawn to seek out another Perfect Master, Upasni Maharaj, a Hindu who lived in Sakori. During the next seven years Maharaj gave Merwan "Gnosis"or Divine Knowledge. Thus Merwan attained spiritual Perfection. His spiritual mission began in 1921 when he drew together his first close disciples. It was these early disciples who gave him the name Meher Baba, which means "Compassionate Father."

After years of intensive training of his disciples, Meher Baba established a colony near Ahmednagar that is called Meherabad. Here the Master's work embraced a free school where spiritual training was stressed, a free hospital and dispensary, and shelters for the poor. No distinction was made between the high castes and the untouchables; all mingled in common fellowship through the inspiration of the Master. To his disciples at Meherabad, who were of different castes and creeds, he gave a training of moral discipline, love for God, spiritual understanding and selfless service.

Meher Baba told his disciples that from July 10, 1925 he would observe Silence. From that day until he dropped the body on January 31, 1969, he maintained this Silence. His many spiritual discourses and messages have been dictated by means of an alphabet board. Much later the Master discontinued the use of the board and reduced all communication to hand gestures unique in expressiveness and understandable to many.

Meher Baba traveled to the Western world six times, first in 1931, when he contacted his early Western disciples. His last visit to America was in 1958 when he and his disciples stayed at the Center established for his work at Myrtle Beach, S.C.

In India as many as one hundred thousand people came in one day to seek his Darshan, or blessing; many from all over the world journeyed to spend a few days, even a single day, in his presence.

An important part of Meher Baba's work through the years was to personally contact and to serve hundreds of those known in India as "masts." These are advanced pilgrims on the spiritual path who have become spiritually intoxicated from direct awareness of God. For this work he traveled many thousands of miles to remote places throughout India and Ceylon. Other vital work was the washing of the lepers, the washing of the feet of thousands of poor and the distribution of grain and cloth to the destitute.

Meher Baba has asserted that he is the same Ancient One, come again to redeem man from his bondage of ignorance and to guide him to realize his true Self which is God. He is acknowledged by his many followers all over the world as the Avatar of the Age. Meher Baba said, "I had to come, and I have come. I am the Ancient One."

Meher Baba said,

*"I had to come
and I have come.
I am the Ancient
One."*

ONE

God and God-Man

Meher Baba has elucidated many of the fine points of the ultimate goal of the creation—God-Realization. He has explained how man becomes God, after the long journey of evolving and involving consciousness; and also how God, uniquely and periodically, becomes man—Avatar, Messiah or Rasool. In essence the consciousness of all Perfect Ones is one and the same; but the burden and duty of the Avatar is greater in circumference. It is for this reason that His effect on the creation, and on mankind in particular, is so profound. The following messages, given at different times, illumine some of these points.*

* For further information, it is suggested one read the *Discourses* and *God Speaks*, by Meher Baba.

God and the Creation

God is infinite reality, whereas cosmos is infine illusion. But both are not infinite in the same sense. God is One Infinite, and illusion is infinite in numbers. God is infinite unity, and Illusion, infinite duality. Always God is. All along Illusion IS NOT. Illusion or no illusion, God remains beginningless and endless, while Illusion has a beginning in illusion and it also ends *in* illusion.

The infinite Illusion includes an infinite number of suns, stars, moons, planets and worlds. The whole of the creation goes on evolving *ad infinitum* in Illusion.

Take for instance the head of a man with innumerable hairs growing over it. When all the hair is shaved off, the growth of hair does not cease; the hairs reappear and cover the head all over again. Even when the head becomes bald, it is only the hair which disappears, the head remains head.

Against the one head, although innumerable, the hairs have next to no value. They may appear and disappear without any difference to the value of the head as such. The value most attached to the hair is but decorative, as a means of attraction and as a lure of self-satisfaction.

Similarly, the individual mind that generates infinite thoughts may be compared with the individual head that has a growth of innumerable hairs. The individual mind is capable of containing, emanating and absorbing an infinite number of thoughts. In fact, all energy and all matter are but the outcome of the mind itself.

To understand the all-importance of God Who is the only Reality, now let us compare Him with the mind, and let the hair over the head be compared to the creation. The illustration would at once suggest that compared with the hair on the head, the mind alone is infinitely valuable. Similarly, I say that God is infinitely valuable when compared with the whole of the creation, which has no value other than that of hair—the hair that lures, and the hair that creates illusory self-satisfaction.

God as Truth

Ultimately every one and every thing is God and that God, as Truth, can be realized through the guru or the Master. Generally in this country, Vedantism is associated with this rendering of the Most High. Now I am not concerned with Vedantism or Sufism or any other "ism," but only with God as Truth, as He comes into our experience, after the disappearance of the limited and limiting ego-mind. God is an unshakable and eternal Truth. He reveals Himself and communicates Himself to those who love Him, seek Him and surrender themselves to Him, either in His *impersonal* aspect, which is beyond name, form and time, or in His *personal* aspect. He is more easily accessible to ordinary man through the God-men, who have always come and will always come, to impart light and truth to struggling humanity, which is groping mostly in darkness.

Because of his complete union with God, the God-man eternally enjoys the "I-am-God" state, which equally corresponds to the Vedantic *Aham Brahmasmi* and the Sufi *Anal-Haq* or Christ's declaration, *"I and my Father are one."* In the experience of the Sufis, *Anal-haq,* or the "I-am-God" state is a culmination of *Hama-Oost,* which means everything is God and nothing else exists. Since in this approach, only "God without a second" is contemplated, there is no room for love for God or longing for God. The soul has the intellectual conviction that it is God. But in order to experience that state actually, it goes through intense concentration or meditation on the thought. *"I am not the body, I am not the mind; I am neither this nor that; I am God."* The soul then experiences through meditation what it has assumed itself to be. But this mode of experiencing God is not only hard but dry.

The Path is more realistic and joyous when there is ample play of love and devotion for God, which postulates temporary and apparent separateness from God and longing to unite with Him. Such *provisional and apparent separateness from God* is affirmed by the soul in the two Sufi conceptions, *Hama az Oost,* which means *Everything is from God* and *Hama Doost,* which means *Everything is for the Beloved God.* In both these conceptions, the soul realizes that its separateness from God is only temporary and apparent and it *seeks to restore this lost unity with God, through intense love which consumes all duality.* The only difference between these two states is that whereas the soul, in the state of *Hama Doost,* rests content with the Will of God as the Beloved, in the state of *Hama az Oost,* the soul longs for nothing but union with God.

Since the soul, which is in bondage, can be redeemed only through Divine Love, even Perfect Masters, who attain complete unity with God and experience Him as the only reality, often apparently step into the domain of duality and talk the language of love, worship and service of God in his Unmanifest Being as well as in all the numberless forms through which He manifests Himself.

Love Divine, as sung by Hindu saints like Tukaram, as taught by Christian mystics like St. Francis, as preached by Zoroastrian saints like Azer Kaivan, and as made immortal by Sufi poets like Hafiz, *harbours no thought of the self at all.* It consumes all wants and frailties, which nourish the bondage and illusion of duality. Ultimately, it *unites the soul with God, thus bringing to the soul true Self-knowledge, abiding happiness, unassailable peace, unbounded understanding and unlimited power.* Be ye inheritors of this *life eternal,* which comes to those who seek!

God as Bliss

Everywhere, in every walk of life, man, without exception, is thirsting for happiness. From the diverse allurements of the sensual life and from the many possessions and attainments that feed and tickle the ego, as also from the numberless experiences which stimulate the intellect, excite the mind, calm down the heart or energize the spirit . . . from all these he seeks happiness of diverse kinds. But he seeks it in the world of duality and in the passing shadows of the Mayavic Illusion, which we call the universe. And he finds that the happiness which he gets therein is so transient that it has almost disappeared in the very moment of experience. And after it disappears, what remains is a bottomless vacuity, which no multiplication of similar experiences can ever completely fill.

But true Bliss can come only to one who would take courage in his hands and become free of all attachment to forms, which are nothing but the illusions of duality. Only then can he get united with his true Beloved, who is God as the eternal and abiding Truth behind all forms, including what he regards as his own body.

The endless and fathomless Ocean of Bliss is within every one. There is no individual who is entirely devoid of happiness in some form; for there is no individual who is entirely cut off from God as the Ocean of Bliss. Every type of pleasure which he ever has is ultimately a partial and illusory reflection of God as *Ananda*. But pleasure, which is sought and experienced in ignorance, ultimately binds the soul to endless continuation of the false life of the ego and leaves the soul exposed to the many sufferings of the ego-life. The pleasures of the illusory world are comparable to the many rivers of mirage that apparently pour themselves into the ocean. *Divine Bliss is ever-fresh, ever-lasting, continuous, and is endlessly experienced as self-sustaining and infinite joy of God.* Be ye united with your Real Beloved, who is God as *Ananda* or Bliss!

The Universal Message

I have come not to teach but to awaken. Understand therefore that I lay down no precepts.

Throughout eternity I have laid down principles and precepts, but mankind has ignored them. Man's inability to live God's words makes the Avatar's teaching a mockery. Instead of practising the compassion He taught, man has waged crusades in His name. Instead of living the humility, purity and truth of His words, man has given way to hatred, greed and violence.

Because man has been deaf to the principles and precepts laid down by God in the past, in this present Avataric Form I observe Silence. You have asked for and been given enough words—it is now time to live them. To get nearer and nearer to God you have to get further and further away from "I," "my," "me" and "mine." You have not to renounce anything but your own self. It is as simple as that, though found to be almost impossible. It is possible for you to renounce your limited self by my Grace. I have come to release that Grace.

I repeat, I lay down no precepts. When I release the tide of Truth which I have come to give, men's daily lives will be the living precept. The words I have not spoken will come to life in them.

I veil myself from man by his own curtain of ignorance, and manifest my Glory to a few. My present Avataric Form is the last incarnation of this cycle of time, hence my Manifestation will be the greatest. When I break my Silence, the impact of my Love will be universal and all life in creation will know, feel and receive of it. It will help every individual to break himself free from his own bondage in his own way. I am the Divine Beloved who loves you more than you can ever love yourself. The breaking of my Silence will help you to help yourself in knowing your real Self.

All this world confusion and chaos was inevitable and no one is to blame. What had to happen has happened; and what has to happen will happen. There was and is no way out except through my coming in your midst. I had to come, and I have come. I am the Ancient One.

The Unconscious Infinite "I"

Due to the Original *Lahar* (whim), the Unconscious Infinite "I" was simultaneously confronted with 1) Consciousness; 2) "Who am I"; and 3) Illusion;—and manifested into innumerable finite "I's," and "said", "I am stone"—"I am metal"—"I am vegetable"—"I am worm"—"I am fish"—"I am bird"—"I am animal"—"I am man"—"I am woman"—"I am body"—"I am energy"—"I am mind"—.

When Illusion disappears, the Infinite "I," with Consciousness retained, says "I am God."

God

In the sub-human stage, the consciousness of false self or false "I," which is very slight, provides scope for evolution. In the human form the evolution of consciousness is completed and the consciousness becomes full. Love comes into play actively for the first time. As love plays the part more actively and fully, the false "I" begins to get consumed more and more. Eventually, when love is at its zenith, the false "I" gets totally consumed by love; this results in consummation of both lover and love at the altar of the Beloved. Neither does the lover remain in love, nor does love reign supreme over the lover: the goal is attained. The Beloved is supreme over his self: there is nothing except the Beloved: everything else is consumed.

Fore-Knowledge

A. The fore-knowledge possessed by an ordinary person depends on memory based on past experiences:

   (a) When a person sees a man on a mountain-top, the person has fore-knowledge that if the man falls down the mountain he will surely die.
   (b) When a person sees a row of horses at the starting point on a race-course, the person has fore-knowledge that the horses will run as soon as the "start" signal is given.
   (c) When a person sees a bottle of whiskey, he has fore-knowledge that the liquid will give intoxication. He associates whiskey with intoxication.

   Thousands of such examples could be given of fore-knowledge in an ordinary person.

B. Fore-knowledge of Perfect Masters (*Qutubs* or *Sadgurus*) depends on the everlasting indivisible experience:

   (a) Everlasting = without break in continuity;
   (b) Everlasting = no scope for past, present and future to determine themselves even relatively.

   Thus it is that Perfect Masters and Avatars assert: "I know everything."

It is due to their *everlasting indivisible experience* that there is *no* scope left for anything other than their infinite, indivisible, omnipresent, all-pervading individual Self (the Existence Eternal).

Omnipresence

There cannot be anything hidden from One who is omnipresent. And as there cannot be hidden anything from such an One, He must be omniscient. He is all-knowing, knowing everything.

Thus, it follows that He must be knowing how to do everything. He will say: I know how to create everything; I know how to destroy everything; I know how to preserve everything; I know how to do everything.

Thus He who is omniscient is inevitably omnipotent. His being omnipresent made Him omniscient and this also made Him omnipotent. In short, to be omnipresent is to be both omniscient and omnipotent simultaneously. All three attributes of God are linked with one another, giving rise to the infinite bliss of God. One who is omnipresent, omniscient and omnipotent, cannot help but be in the infinitely blissful state.

On Being The Avatar

When I say I am the Avatar, there are a few who feel happy, some who feel shocked, and many who, hearing me claim this, would take me for a hypocrite, a fraud, a supreme egoist, or just mad. If I were to say every one of you is an Avatar, a few would be tickled, and many would consider it a blasphemy or a joke. The fact that God being One, indivisible, and equally in us all, we can be nought else but one, is too much for the duality-conscious mind to accept. Yet each of us is what the other is. I know I am the Avatar in every sense of the word, and that each of you is an Avatar in one sense or the other.

It is an unalterable and universally recognized fact since time immemorial that God knows everything, God does everything, and that nothing happens but by the will of God. Therefore it is God who makes me say I am the

Avatar, and that each one of you is an Avatar. Again, it is He who is tickled through some, and through others is shocked. It is God who acts and God who reacts. It is He who scoffs and He who responds. He is the Creator, the Producer, the Actor and the Audience in His own Divine Play.

On Being Silent

If you were to ask me why I do not speak, I would say I am not silent, and that I speak more eloquently through gestures and the alphabet board.

If you were to ask me why I do not talk, I would say, perhaps for three reasons. Firstly, I feel that through you all I am talking eternally. Secondly, to relieve the boredom of talking incessantly through your forms, I keep silence in my personal physical form. And thirdly, because all talk, in itself, is idle talk. Lectures, messages, statements, discourses of any kind, spiritual or otherwise, imparted through utterances or writings, is just idle talk when not acted upon or lived up to.

If you were to ask when I will break my Silence, I would say when I feel like uttering the only real Word that was spoken in the beginningless beginning, as that Word alone is worth uttering. The time for the breaking of my outward Silence to utter that Word, is very near.

Meher Baba's Call

Age after age, when the wick of Righteousness burns low, the Avatar comes yet once again to rekindle the torch of Love and Truth. Age after age, amidst the clamour of disruptions, wars, fear and chaos, rings the Avatar's call: *"Come all unto me."*

Although, because of the veil of illusion, this Call of the Ancient One may appear as a voice in the wilderness, its echo and re-echo nevertheless pervades through time and space, to rouse at first a few, and eventually millions, from their deep slumber of ignorance. And in the midst of illusion, as the Voice behind all voices, it awakens humanity to bear witness to the manifestation of God amidst mankind.

The time is come. I repeat the Call, and bid all come unto me.

This time-honored Call of mine thrills the hearts of those who have patiently endured all in their love for God, loving God only for love of God. There are those who fear and shudder at its reverberations, and would flee or resist. And there are yet others who, baffled, fail to understand why the Highest of the High, who is all-sufficient, need necessarily give this Call to humanity.

Irrespective of doubts and convictions, and for the Infinite Love I bear for one and all, I continue to come as the Avatar, to be judged time and again by humanity in its ignorance, in order to help man distinguish the Real from the false.

Invariably muffled in the cloak of the infinitely true humility of the Ancient One, the Divine Call is at first little heeded, until, in its Infinite strength it spreads in volume to reverberate and keep on reverberating in countless hearts as the Voice of Reality.

Strength begets humility, whereas modesty bespeaks weakness. Only he who is truly great can *be* really humble.

When, in the firm knowledge of it, a man admits his true greatness, it is in itself an expression of humility. He accepts his greatness as most natural and is expressing merely what he is, just as a man would not hesitate to admit to himself and others the fact of his being man.

For a truly great man, who knows himself to be truly great, to deny his greatness would be to belittle what he indubitably is. For whereas modesty is the basis of guise, true greatness is free from camouflage.

On the other hand, when a man expresses a greatness he knows or feels he does not possess, he is the greatest hypocrite.

Honest is the man who is not great, and, knowing and feeling this, firmly and frankly states that he is not great.

There are more than a few who are not great, yet assume a humility in the genuine belief of their own worth. Through words and actions they express repeatedly their humbleness, professing to be servants of humanity. True humility is not acquired by merely donning a garb of humility. True humility spontaneously and continually emanates from the strength of the truly great. Voicing one's humbleness does not make one humble. For all that a parrot may utter, "I am a man," it does not make it so.

Better the absence of greatness than the establishing of a false greatness by assumed humility. Not only do these efforts at humility on man's part not express strength, they are, on the contrary, expressions of modesty born of weakness, which springs from a lack of knowledge of the truth of Reality.

Beware of modesty. Modesty, under the cloak of humility, invariably leads one into the clutches of self-deception. Modesty breeds egoism and man eventually succumbs to pride through assumed humility.

The greatest greatness and the greatest humility go hand in hand naturally and without effort.

When the Greatest of all says, "I am the Greatest," it is but a spontaneous expression of an infallible Truth. The strength of His greatness lies, not in raising the dead, but in His great humiliation when He allows Himself to be ridiculed, persecuted and crucified at the hands of those who are weak in flesh and spirit. Throughout the ages, humanity has failed to fathom the true depth of the humility underlying the greatness of the Avatar, gauging his divinity by its acquired limited religious standards. Even real saints and sages, who have some knowledge of the Truth, have failed to understand the Avatar's greatness when faced with his real humility.

Age after age history repeats itself when men and women, in their ignorance, limitations and pride, sit in judgment over the God-incarnated man who declares his Godhood, and condemn him for uttering the Truths they cannot understand. He is indifferent to abuse and persecution for, in His true compassion He understands, in His continual experience of Reality He knows, and in His infinite mercy He forgives.

God is all. God knows all, and God does all. When the Avatar proclaims he is the Ancient One, it is God who proclaims His manifestation on earth. When man utters for or against the Avatarhood it is God who speaks through him. It is God alone who declares Himself through the Avatar and mankind.

THE PATH OF LOVE

I tell you all with my Divine authority, that you and I are not "we," but "one." You unconsciously feel my Avatarhood within you; I consciously feel in you what each of you feel. Thus every one of us is Avatar, in the sense that everyone and everything is everyone and everything, at the same time, and for all time.

There is nothing but God. He is the only Reality, and we all are one in the indivisible Oneness of this absolute Reality. When the One who has realized God says, "I am God. You are God, and we are all one," and also awakens this feeling of Oneness in His illusion-bound selves, then the question of the lowly and the great, the poor and the rich, the humble and the modest, the good and the bad, simply vanishes. It is his false awareness of duality that misleads man into making illusory distinctions and filing them into separate categories.

I repeat and emphasize that in my continual and eternal experience of Reality, no difference exists between the worldly rich and the poor. But, if ever such a question of difference between opulence and poverty were to exist for me, I would deem him really poor who, possessing worldly riches, possesses not the wealth of Love for God. And, I would know him truly rich who, owning nothing, possesses the priceless treasure of his Love for God. His is the poverty that kings could envy, and that makes even the King of kings his slave.

Know therefore, that in the eyes of God, the only difference between the rich and the poor is not of wealth and poverty, but in the degrees of intensity and sincerity in the longing for God.

Love for God alone can annihilate the falsity of the limited ego, the basis of the life ephemeral. It alone can make one realize the Reality of one's Unlimited Ego, the basis of Eternal Existence. The divine Ego, as the basis of Eternal Existence, continually expresses Itself; but, shrouded in the veil of ignorance, man misconstrues his Indivisible Ego and experiences and expresses it as the limited, separate ego.

Pay heed when I say with my Divine Authority, that the Oneness of Reality is so uncompromisingly Unlimited and All-pervading that not only "We are one," but even this collective term of "we" has no place in the

Infinite Indivisible Oneness.

Awaken from your ignorance, and try at least to understand that in the uncompromisingly Indivisible Oneness, not only is the Avatar God, but also the ant and the sparrow, just as one and all of you are nothing but God. The only apparent difference is in the states of consciousness. The Avatar knows that that which is a sparrow is not a sparrow, whereas the sparrow does not realize this, and, being ignorant of its ignorance, identifies itself as a sparrow.

Live not in ignorance. Do not waste your precious life-span in differentiating and judging your fellow-men, but learn to long for the love of God. Even in the midst of your worldly activities, live only to find and realize your true Identity with your Beloved God.

Be pure and simple, and love all because all are one. Live a sincere life; be natural, and be honest with yourself.

Honesty will guard you against false modesty and will give you the strength of true humility. Spare no pains to help others. Seek no other reward than the gift of Divine Love. Yearn for this gift sincerely and intensely, and I promise in the name of my Divine Honesty, that I will give you much more than you yearn for.

I give you all my blessing that the spark of my Divine Love may implant in your hearts the deep longing for Love of God.

I Am the Son of God the Father and God the Mother in One

God is One. He is both father and mother in One. He is in everyone and in everything; but God is beyond this too. I will tell you about God in the Beyond state. In the Beyond state God is both God the father and God the mother simultaneously.

Now we will discuss the worldly father and mother. Suppose a couple has seven sons. It is natural for the father to love those sons who are useful to him, who are healthy, intelligent, brilliant—obviously, the father will remain pleased with such sons. Now the six sons of this worldly father are healthy, strong, intelligent and good in all respects; the seventh son is a disabled weakling, innocent, simple and guileless (*Bhola*). The father has no love for this seventh son and loves only his six sons. But the mother loves her seventh son the most; more so, because he is weak, sick, disabled, simple and guileless.

God is both the father and the mother in One. The Avatars are Sons of the Father in the Beyond state. All past Avataric periods witnessed the presence of the Avatar as the healthy, bright, wise Son of God. All this means that the Avatar always remained the Beloved Son of the Father. Note that the Avatar always takes a male form and mingles with mankind as man.

Hitherto, God in the Beyond state did not have occasion to play the part of God the mother. In this Avataric period, God the Father is very pleased with me at my being infinitely bright, wise, efficient and perfect in all respects (*Ustad* or "shrewd") as my Father wants me to be; and I am the beloved Son of my Father. At the same time, in this form I am physically disabled. In America, in 1952, I was injured on the left side of my physical frame from leg to face. In India, in 1956, I injured my right side from the head down to the leg. Besides being physically disabled I am also infinitely simple and guileless (*Bhola*). Thus, I am also the well-beloved Son of my God the Mother. So, in this Incarnation of the Avatar, God has the occasion, as it were, to play the part of both father and mother.

There Is Only ONE

In the Beyond-State of God, sex does not exist. There, only the One, Indivisible Existence prevails. It is in the realm of the illusory phenomenon called the universe, that sex asserts itself.

Babajan, the Perfect Master, who in less than an instant, made me experience my Ancient Infinite State, had the Muslim-form of a woman. Upasni Maharaj, who brought me down to normal consciousness, had the Hindu-form of a man. As a young and beautiful girl, Babajan, who was of a noble and rich family, renounced the world just before she was going to be married, because of her great love for God and the urge to be One with God.

It was at Poona, with one kiss on my forehead, that Babajan made me know that I am the Ancient One. She was then about an hundred years old, sitting under a tree like a true *Faquir*.

Every one of you, man or woman, of any caste, creed, or colour, has an equal right to attain Divinity. It has been possible for man to become God through love of God. External renunciation is not at all necessary. Each and all, man or woman, whilst attending to all duties in the everyday walk of life, can attain to Divine Fatherhood and Universal Motherhood through honest love for God.

To express your love for God, you must live a life of love, honesty and self-sacrifice. Merely to chant the *Arti*,* to perform *Puja*,* to offer flowers, fruits and sweets and to bow down, can never mean that you love God as He ought to be loved.

Similarly, merely giving *darshan* to masses, having crowds flocking around, delivering messages to multitudes, and performing so-called miracles may be conventionally accepted attributes of a Divine Personage in your midst, but I say with Divine Honesty that all this is not necessarily a sign of true Divinity.

God is not to be lured, but is to be loved. God is not to be preached, but is to be lived. Only those who live the life of love, honesty and self-sacrifice, can know me as the Ancient One.

I can say with Divine Authority that I experience eternally, consciously and continually, being One with you all, and One in you all. Any worship or obedience to any deity—animate or inanimate—to any saint, master, advanced soul, or yogi, eventually comes to me. By offering pure unadulterated love to anyone and to anything you will be loving me, as I am in every one and in everything, and also beyond everything.

I want you all to know that whatever you do, good or bad, the one thing not forgiven by God is to pose as that which you really are not.

*Hindu prayer ceremonies

With Divine Authority I repeat that we are all One. Being rich or poor, literate or illiterate, or high caste or low caste, need not interfere with your loving God—the Supreme Beloved.

I give you all my blessings for the understanding that loving God, in any form, in any way, will make you eternally FREE.

The Circles of the Avatar

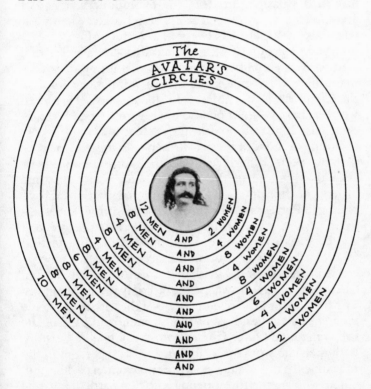

Absolute oneness prevails in Reality. Space and time are but illusory. They are merely the effect of the reflection of God's Infinitude. When man realizes Reality, the reflection which has estranged him from Reality, vanishes, and he experiences the absoluteness of the Absolute Oneness of God. And, when such a man continues to live his life in illusion, he leads the life of the Man-God or Perfect Master on earth. With his abiding experience of the Absolute Reality, he serves as the pivot around which rotates the entire cosmic universe. Every point in the cosmos is equidistant from the Perfect Master, who abides in illusion as the nucleus of the cosmos.

Although the Perfect Master remains in illusion as the center of the cosmic periphery, and radiates his influence uniformly over the entire universe, in his lifetime he gathers round him twelve men to directly have their center of interest in his individuality. These men, through their constant and close association with him in the past, right from the evolutionary stages of consciousness, reap the greatest benefit now when their past close associate has become a Perfect Master.

Such a group of 12 men is called the "Circle" of a Perfect Master. However, besides this group of twelve men, there is an appendage of two women to complete the Circle of a Perfect Master in all its aspects. These two women also owe their position in regard to the Circle, to their past connection with the Perfect Master.

One or more of these fourteen close ones associated with the Perfect Master realizes the God-state during or after the lifetime of the Perfect Master; and in some instances, after one or a few more reincarnations. However, the Perfect Master fulfills his obligations by establishing his Circle during his lifetime, and the greatest good he bestows is God-realization with all its Perfection to at least one from among his circle of twelve men.

In the case of the Avatar it is different. He has ten Circles in all, as shown in the accompanying diagram. The first or Inner Circle of the Avatar consists of twelve men with an appendage of two women; and each of the following nine Outer Circles consists of twelve persons, both men and women. In all there are 120 persons in the ten circles of the Avatar, plus the two women of the Inner Circle who are but the appendage to that particular Circle (122 in all).

Either one or more of the 108 members of the nine Outer Circles realize the God-state during or after the life-span of the Avatar; and some in the next incarnation or after a few more reincarnations.

As in the case of the Perfect Master's Circle, the Inner Circle of the Avatar consists of only twelve men, with an appendage of two women. The difference between the Circle of the Perfect Master and the Inner Circle of the Avatar is that the Perfect Master *establishes* his Circle from amongst those who were closely connected with him right from the evolutionary stages of their consciousness; but the Avatar who, in his recurrent advents, neither passes through the process of evolution, reincarnation, nor involution, does not therefore have the same links of association to establish anew his Inner Circle with every advent. In short, whereas the Perfect Master establishes his Circle, the Avatar is directly allied with his Inner Circle, which is always the same in all his advents. With his descent on earth, the Avatar, as it were, brings along with him the association of his Inner Circle.

The connection of the Inner Circle in relation to the Avatar may be compared to that of a man who directly associates himself with the fourteen parts of his own body: two eyes, two ears, two nostrils, one mouth, two hands, two legs, and the trunk of the body itself; plus the external genitals and anus that act as the appendage to the body as a whole. As soon as man is born, he directly makes use of these fourteen parts of his body, and these parts in turn respond to his dictates individually or collectively.

Similarly, with the advent of the Avatar on earth, His Inner Circle of the same twelve individualities and the appendage of the same two individualities directly begin to function, individually and collectively, according to the dictates of the Avatar himself.

With every advent of the Avatar on earth, the 12 men of the Inner Circle and its appendage of two women, gather round the personality of the Avatar, as the self-same 14 types of individualities. These fourteen different individualities, *in the shape of different personalities,* always occupy their respective offices, whenever the Avatar manifests on earth; and during and after the life-span of the Avatar, they—individually and collectively—function in the same way as their predecessors, who had held, and functioned in, the same offices of the Inner Circle during the past advents of the Avatar.

Therefore it would *not* be wrong to say that with Christ's coming again, come Peter, Judas, and all his apostles. But this can never mean that the *very same* Peter, or the self-same Judas, reincarnates again and again. These can never reincarnate, as all of the twelve individual personalities of the Avatar's Inner Circle attain God-realization in every Avataric period, either during or soon after the life-span of the Avatar.

Once God-realization is attained, reincarnation is impossible. The only exception to this rule is the Avatar himself, who comes again and again to redeem humanity.

It is not the same individualized personalities of the Inner Circle that reincarnate; it is the *individualities of their particular offices* that come with every advent of the Avatar. It is because in all the Avatar's advents each of the twelve men and two women of the Inner Circle hold exactly the same office and function in exactly the same manner, that it is said the Avatar always brings with him the same Circle.

As soon as the veil, with which the Avatar descends on earth, is rent, by the then-living Perfect Master or Masters, and the Avatar realizes his Avatarhood, the twelve men and two women automatically group round the personality of the Avatar to occupy their respective positions in the Inner Circle and to function as usual according to the dictates of the Avatar of the Age.

The position of the Avatar in regard to the Inner Circle and its function may be compared to a man asleep. As soon as the man is made to wake up through some external agency, and no sooner is he awake, than he spontaneously finds that all the fourteen parts of his body, as mentioned before, are already there in their individual roles, ready to function at the slightest wish of the man. Similarly, as soon as the Avatar is made to realize his Avatarhood through one or two or more of the five Perfect Masters of the time, he also realizes that the 14 personalities, in their characteristic roles of the Inner Circle, are ready at hand to discharge their duties.

To explain in detail why only these 14 particular personalities hold such positions in every advent of the Avatar would take a volume of explanations. Who can become the fourteen members and how do they become attached to the Inner Circle of the Avatar?—these questions would require more volumes of explanation.

Suffice it to say that each of these fourteen particular

personalities, when occupying the office and function of the Inner Circle, not only must resemble the characteristic individuality of his or her predecessor in the previous advents of the Avatar, but must be exactly similar in all respects. For example, one of the offices of the Inner Circle of Jesus Christ was held by Peter. At the second advent of Christ, this particular office must be held by another Peter, who may be named "A," but having the same quality of mind and heart and other characteristics as of *the Peter*. The same applies to the office held by Judas, John, James, etc., of the Inner Circle in the time of Christ.

All fourteen members of the Avatar's Inner Circle realize God by the grace of the Avatar, during the same Avataric period, which is of one hundred years' duration after the Manifestation of the Avatar on earth.

Regarding the Outer Circles of the Avatar, none of the 108 persons in the nine circles holds any office similar to that held by those of the Inner Circle; and all of these 108 persons attain God-realization by the grace of the Avatar, but not necessarily during the Avataric period.

These 108 persons of the Outer Circle have their respective places in the nine Circles in accordance with their past connections with the members of the Circle ahead of them. For example, the members of the Second Circle of twelve persons, next to the Inner Circle, are grouped round the Avatar in accordance with their past connections with the members of the Inner Circle. Similarly, the twelve persons of the Third Circle, next to the second Circle, are grouped round the Avatar in accordance with their past connections with the members of the Second Circle; and so on, with all the remaining seven Circles.

Action and Inaction

I. In the Beyond-Beyond state of God there is: "Unconscious Inaction."

II. In the state of God-realization, there is: "Conscious Inaction."
    This is not the state of Perfection but of Liberation (*Najaat*). In this state there is absolute tranquility

which gives rise to infinite power, knowledge and bliss.

III. In the Intermediate state (between I & II) there is: "Conscious Action."

Actions promote *sanskaras* (impressions). *Sanskaras* in turn breed more actions and create bindings: in this state there is bondage.

IV. In the state of a *Majzoob* of a 7th plane there is: "Unconscious Action."

V. In the state of Perfect Masters there is: "Conscious Active Inaction."

Perfect Masters are free of *sanskaras*: they have no impressions. As such, there cannot be room for actions of their own: their life is one of inaction but made active because of the prevailing environmental circumstances. Actions of Perfect Masters are prompted by the environment-atmosphere prevailing then.

EXAMPLES:

I. The Beyond-Beyond state of God may be compared with a child fast asleep in a cradle: it is an example of "Unconscious Inaction."

II. The state of the God-realized person (not a Perfect Master) may be compared with a child wide awake but still in the cradle: this is an example of "Conscious Inaction."

III. The state in between I & II may be compared with a child awake and out of the cradle: it is an example of "Conscious Action."

IV. The state of a *Majzoob* of a 7th plane may be compared with a somnambulist: the somnambulist walks about or performs other actions in sleep and is not aware of what he does in this state. Similarly the *Majzoob* of the 7th plane does actions and is not conscious of them. His is "Unconscious Action": he eats, drinks, speaks, etc. But all this is his "Unconscious Action."

V. The state of a Perfect Master may be compared with a child wide awake but inside the cradle that is continuously rocked by mankind. It is "Conscious Active Inaction." Inaction is being inside the cradle: and active inaction is the rocking of the cradle by others.

God is Conscious Inaction indeed. And the tranquility of this "Conscious Inaction" is so very profound that it gives God the attributes of Infinite Power, Infinite Knowledge and Infinite Bliss.

The Highest of The High

Consciously or unconsciously, directly or indirectly, each and every creature, each and every human being strives to assert individuality. When eventually man consciously experiences that he is Infinite, Eternal and Indivisible, he is fully conscious of his individuality as God, and experiences Infinite Knowledge, Infinite Power and Infinite Bliss. Thus Man becomes God, and is recognized as a Perfect Master, *Sadguru,* or *Qutub.*

When God manifests on earth in the form of man and reveals his Divinity to mankind, he is recognized as the Avatar—thus God becomes Man.

And so Infinite God, age after age, throughout all cycles, wills through His Infinite Mercy to effect His presence amidst mankind by stooping down to human level in the human form, but His physical presence amidst mankind not being apprehended, He is looked upon as an ordinary man of the world. When He asserts, however, His Divinity on earth by proclaiming Himself the Avatar of the age, He is worshipped by some who accept Him as God; and glorified by a few who know him as God on Earth. But it invariably falls to the lot of the rest of humanity to condemn Him, while He is physically in their midst.

Thus it is that God as man, proclaiming Himself as the Avatar, suffers Himself to be persecuted and tortured, to be humiliated and condemned by humanity for whose sake His Infinite Love has made him stoop so low, in order that humanity, by its very act of condemning God's manifestation in the form of Avatar should, however, indirectly, assert the existence of God in His Infinite Eternal state.

The Avatar is always one and the same, because God is always One and the Same, the Eternal, Indivisible, Infinite One, who manifests himself in the form of man as the Avatar, as the Messiah, as the Prophet, as the Ancient One—the Highest of the High. This Eternally One and the Same Avatar repeats his manifestation from time to time, in different cycles, adopting different human forms and different names, in different places, to reveal Truth in different garbs and different languages, in order to raise humanity from the pit of ignorance and free it from the bondage of delusions.

Of the most recognized and much worshipped manifestations of God as Avatar, that of Zoroaster is the earlier—having been before Rama, Krishna, Buddha, Jesus and Muhammad. Thousands of years ago, he gave to the world the essence of Truth in the form of three fundamental precepts—Good Thoughts, Good Words, and Good Deeds. These precepts were and are constantly unfolded to humanity in one form or another, directly or indirectly in every cycle, by the Avatar of the Age, as he leads humanity towards the Truth. To put these precepts of Good Thoughts, Good Words and Good Deeds into practice is not easily done, though it is not impossible. But to live up to these precepts honestly and literally is apparently as impossible as it is to practise a living death in the midst of life.

In the world there are countless *sadhus, mahatmas, mahapurushas,* saints, yogis and *walis,* though the number of genuine ones is very, very limited. The few genuine ones are, according to their spiritual status, in a category of their own, which is neither on a level with the ordinary human being nor on a level with the state of the Highest of the High.

I am neither a *mahatma* nor a *mahapurush,* neither a *sadhu* nor a saint, neither a yogi nor a *wali.* Those who approach me with the desire to gain wealth or to retain their possessions, those who seek through me relief from distress and suffering, those who ask my help to fulfil and satisfy mundane desires, to them I once again declare that, as I am not a *sadhu,* a saint or a *mahatma, mahapurush* or yogi, to seek these things through me is but to court utter disappointment, though only apparently; for eventually the disappointment is itself instrumental in bringing about the complete transformation of mundane wants and desires.

The *sadhus,* saints, yogis, *walis* and such others who are on the *via media,** can and do perform miracles and

---

* The Middle Path

satisfy the transient material needs of individuals who approach them for help and relief.

The question therefore arises that if I am not a *sadhu,* not a saint, not a yogi, not a *mahapurush* nor a *wali,* then what am I? The natural assumption would be that I am either just an ordinary human being, or I am the Highest of the High. But one thing I say definitely, and that is that I can never be included amongst those having the intermediary status of the real *sadhus,* saints, yogis and such others.

Now, if I am just an ordinary man, my capabilities and powers are limited—I am no better or different from an ordinary human being. If people take me as such they should not expect supernatural help from me in the form of miracles or spiritual guidance; and to approach me to fulfil their desires would also be absolutely futile.

On the other hand, if I am beyond the level of an ordinary human being, and much beyond the level of saints and yogis, then I must be the Highest of the High. In which case, to judge me with your human intellect and limited mind and to approach me with mundane desires would not only be the height of folly but sheer ignorance as well; because no amount of intellectual effort could ever understand my ways or judge my Infinite State.

If I am the Highest of the High, my Will is Law, my wish governs the Law, and my Love sustains the Universe. Whatever your apparent calamities and transient sufferings, they are but the outcome of my Love for the ultimate good. Therefore, to approach me for deliverance from your predicaments, to expect me to satisfy your worldly desires, would be asking me to do the impossible—to undo what I have already ordained.

If you truly and in all faith accept your Baba as the Highest of the High, it behooves you to lay down your life at his feet, rather than to crave the fulfilment of your desires. Not your one life but your millions of lives would be but a small sacrifice to place at the feet of One such as Baba, who is the Highest of the High; for Baba's unbounded love is the only sure and unfailing guide to lead you safely through the innumerable blind alleys of your transient life.

They cannot obligate me, who, surrendering their all—(body, mind, possessions)—which perforce they must discard one day—surrender with a motive; surrender because they understand that to gain the everlasting treasure of Bliss they must relinquish ephemeral possessions. This desire for greater gain is still clinging behind their surrender, and as such the surrender cannot be complete.

Know you all that if I am the Highest of the High, my role demands that I strip you of all your possessions and wants, consume all your desires and make you desireless rather than satisfy your desires. *Sadhus,* saints, yogis and *walis* can give you what you want; but I take away your wants and free you from attachments and liberate you from the bondage of ignorance. I am the One to take, not the One to give what you want or as you want.

Mere intellectuals can never understand me through their intellect. If I am the Highest of the High, it becomes impossible for the mind to gauge me nor is it possible for my ways to be fathomed by the human mind.

I am not to be attained by those who, loving me, stand reverently by in rapt admiration. I am not for those who ridicule me and point at me with contempt. To have a crowd of tens of millions flocking around me is not what I am for. I am for the few who, scattered amongst the crowd, silently and unostentatiously surrender their all—body, mind and possessions—to me. I am still more for those who, after surrendering their all, never give another thought to their surrender. They are all mine who are prepared to renounce even the very thought of their renunciation and who, keeping constant vigil in the midst of intense activity, await their turn to lay down their lives for the cause of Truth at a glance or sign from me. Those who have indomitable courage to face willingly and cheerfully the worst calamities, who have unshakable faith in me, eager to fulfil my slightest wish at the cost of their happiness and comfort, they indeed, truly love me.

From my point of view, far more blessed is the atheist who confidently discharges his worldly responsibilities, accepting them as his honourable duty, than the man who presumes he is a devout believer in God, yet shirks the responsibilities apportioned to him through

Divine Law and runs after *sadhus,* saints and yogis, seeking relief from the suffering which ultimately would have pronounced his eternal liberation.

To have one eye glued on the enchanting pleasures of the flesh and with the other expect to see a spark of Eternal Bliss is not only impossible but the height of hypocrisy.

I cannot expect you to understand all at once what I want you to know. It is for me to awaken you from time to time throughout the ages, sowing the seed in your limited minds, which must in due course and with proper heed and care on your part, germinate, flourish and bear the fruit of that True Knowledge which is inherently yours to gain.

If on the other hand, led by your ignorance, you persist in going your own way, none can stop you in your choice of progress; for that too is progress which, however slow and painful, eventually and after innumerable re-incarnations, is bound to make you realize that which I want you to know *now.* To save yourself from further entanglement in the maze of delusion and self-created suffering, which owes its magnitude to the extent of your ignorance of the true Goal, *awake now.* Pay heed and strive for Freedom by experiencing ignorance in its true perspective. Be honest with yourself and God. One may fool the world and one's neighbours, but one can never escape from the knowledge of the Omniscient—such is the Divine Law.

I declare to all of you who approach me, and to those of you who desire to approach me, accepting me as the Highest of the High, that you must never come with the desire in your heart which craves for wealth and worldly gain, but only with the fervent longing to give your all—body, mind and possessions—with all their attachments. Seek me not to extricate you from your predicaments, but find me in order to surrender yourself wholeheartedly to my Will. Cling to me not for worldly happiness and short-lived comforts, but adhere to me, through thick and thin, sacrificing your own happiness and comforts at my feet. Let my happiness be your cheer and my comfort your rest. Do not ask me to bless you with a good job, but desire to serve me more diligently and honestly without expectation of reward. Never beg of me to save your life or the lives of your dear ones, but beg of me to accept you and permit you to lay down your life for me. Never expect me to cure you of your bodily afflictions, but beseech me to cure you of your ignorance. Never stretch out your hands to receive anything from me, but hold them high in praise of me whom you have approached as the Highest of the High.

If I am then the Highest of the High, nothing is impossible to me; and though I do not perform miracles to satisfy individual needs—the satisfaction of which would result in entangling the individual more and more in the net of ephemeral existence—yet time and again at certain periods I manifest the Infinite Power in the form of miracles, but only for the spiritual upliftment and benefit of humanity and all creatures.

However, miraculous experiences have often been experienced by individuals who love me and have unswerving faith in me, and these have been attributed to my *nazar* or Grace on them. But I want all to know that it does not befit my lovers to attribute such individual miraculous experiences to my state of the Highest of the High. If I am the Highest of the High I am above these illusory plays of *maya* in the course of the Divine Law. Therefore, whatever miraculous experiences are experienced by my lovers who recognize me as such, or by those who love me unknowingly through other channels, they are but the outcome of their own firm faith in me. Their unshakable faith, often superseding the course of the play of *maya,* gives them those experiences which they call miracles. Such experiences derived through firm faith eventually do good and do not entangle the individuals who experience them in further and greater bindings of Illusion.

If I am the Highest of the High, then a wish of my Universal Will is sufficient to give, in an instant, God-realization to one and all, and thus free every creature in creation from the shackles of Ignorance. But blessed is Knowledge that is gained through the experience of Ignorance, in accordance with the Divine Law. This Knowledge is made possible for you to attain in the midst of Ignorance by the guidance of Perfect Masters and by surrender to the Highest of the High.

TWO
Aspects of the Path

There are many roads, but only one Path. Once consciousness, in man, is full, it must experience every aspect of life, through many incarnations. And once consciousness is full of experience, it inevitably reaches the turning point, and begins to seek its Source. The prodigal soul must return to its Father, and start the homeward journey. This is essentially a journey through self towards the real Self, towards God, and union with Him. It is on this return journey, a journey still in illusion, but through the brilliant illusion of the spiritual Planes, that we seek the guidance of One who knows the way.

Baba Explains

ABOUT MIRACLES . . .
Why should we produce petty imitation illusions in the already created mighty Infinite Illusion?

Unless absolutely necessary, for the spiritual purpose of a general collective drawing of mankind towards Self-realization, miracles performed unnaturally or supernaturally can interfere with GOD's ordained evolutionary process.

ABOUT HEALING . . .
Real healing is spiritual healing, whereby the soul, becoming free from desires, doubts and hallucinations, enjoys the eternal bliss of GOD.

Untimely physical healing might retard the spiritual healing. If borne willingly, physical and mental suffering can make one worthy of receiving spiritual healing. Consider mental and physical suffering as gifts from GOD, which, if accepted gracefully, lead to everlasting happiness.

ABOUT SILENCE . . .
God has been everlastingly working in silence, unobserved, unheard, except by those who experience His Infinite Silence.

If my Silence cannot speak, of what avail would be speeches made by the tongue?

The very moment when He thinks my speaking would be heard universally, GOD will make me break my Silence.

Knowledge and Imagination

On the one hand, Divine Knowledge (*Dnyan* or *Marefat*) is a thing which cannot be had even after going through numberless forms for countless ages; and on the other hand, when it comes, it comes. It would not be correct to say that Knowledge comes quickly. To say that it comes suddenly, or that it comes unawares and so on still does not correctly express the "Flash of Becoming" which is beyond description, because Knowledge is *beyond the range of imagination.*

Imagination has a tremendous range and an almost unlimited scope and man has a very strong imagination. For example, it would not be impossible for a man to imagine a rat having a million heads. The whole world is created and carried on by the force of the imagination. But in spite of being apparently unlimited, imagination reaches the limit when checked by Knowledge itself. By the power of imagination no man can ever understand or explain the beginningless beginning or the endless end. In other words, Eternity is beyond the reach of all imagination, and Knowledge is Knowledge of Eternity.

God is without beginning and without end, and there can never be any question of time and space in Infinity as, otherwise, that would mean a limitation against God's infinitude. No amount of imagination can, therefore, ever think of Infinity, because where there is no beginning, the very question as to what was in the beginning cannot arise at all.

For example, let us repeat that before God, there was God, and before that, there was God, and before that there was God; or repeat that after God, is God, and after that, God is, and after that God is: and all this would convey nothing to the imagination. That is why Knowledge is said to be even beyond the reach of Rishis and Munis (the advanced Saints). Hafiz also advises against the futility of trying to catch the "Falcon" of Knowledge when he says that nothing but "emptiness" can ever come into the "net of imagination."

Thus, the most powerful mind in imagination is entirely helpless against Knowledge, because it comes only after all power of imagination is completely and absolutely exhausted and ended. For imagination to go, mind must go; and for Knowledge to come, consciousness must remain. Only when the mind disappears does consciousness get freed of all imaginary "this and that" and "I and you." The moment consciousness is freed from all imagination, this "consciousness of nothing" is all at once transformed into the "Knowledge of Everything," i.e., *Dnyan* or *Marefat*.

Even Vedanta and Sufism cannot reach or explain Knowledge. One may try to imagine a shoreless ocean with numberless drops, and think of it in various terms of comparison and contrast, but just as "no beginning—no end" would always remain "no beginning—no end," so, Knowledge can never be imagined. If that be so, and if I were a listener amongst you, I would have asked "Then why all this headache over explaining a thing which can neither be explained nor grasped?"

Ordinary *Swayambhu*-Knowledge or the ordinary self-knowledge does not depend upon any process of reasoning or imagination. A man, woman or child neither acquires nor has any need to acquire the knowledge of one's individual existence from sources outside existence itself. A woman knows that she is a woman. This knowledge is not received. It is self-knowledge of womanhood; and the same is the case with the self-knowledge of manhood and childhood for a man and a child.

Similarly, Divine *Swayambhu*-Knowledge is Divine Knowledge of Power, Beauty and Bliss. When one gets such *Dnyan* or *Irfaan,* one not only feels oneself in every one and in every thing, but one then actually lives the free life of God. This Knowledge can come even at a moment when one is attending to a call of nature, as has actually happened in certain cases, including that of Upasni Maharaj. That is because a Master can give Knowledge any moment, instantaneously, provided there is sufficiently deep and strong connection with him, or there is complete surrender to his will. The only other way is complete annihilation of "imagination," like the attempt to prove that "nothing" is really "nothing," which amounts to the annihilation of a mind by itself and as such, it is next to impossible.

Granting that as a very, very rare case, a man succeeds in breaking through his imagination by himself and achieves union with the Truth, still, such a one cannot make any use of the knowledge and so he can not become a *Dnyani* or *A'riff.* That is why Masters like Tukaram and Dnyaneshwar, Hafiz and Rumi, all say that there is no way out of imagination or ignorance, except with the help and by the Grace of a Perfect Master.

The fact is that God alone is real, and every thing is in God. We all are one with Him, but owing to our ignorance, we feel ourselves separate from God. We always were. What was before us? We. Before "we?" We! We! We! Only when we get Knowledge, we know what this *BEING* means. Then instantly, everything is absolutely clear in the twinkling of an eye; but such a "Flash of

Being" is even quicker than the twinkling of an eye! There is therefore no question of becoming God, since we are already God; and so, on the other hand, we have to cease to be God. In order to do that, we have got to get more and more away from God through prayers, fasting, etc., as otherwise, what can God do for God?

That is why Knowledge cannot come to one and all individuals because we all are God, and God being in every one, who is to give and to whom? Only when God is perfectly Individualized as Most Perfect *Dnyani* or Most Perfect *A'riff,* can he impart Knowledge to other individuals. The question may yet be asked as to why should the Master then not impart Knowledge to all individuals instead of giving Knowledge to some, and not giving it to others?

This is a question of Law Divine, commonly known as the Law of Karma, or Law of Bindings, or Law of Cause and Effect. Except the Perfect *Dnyani* or Perfect *A'riff,* no other individual can under any circumstances escape this law and its consequences. Therefore when the Master gives Knowledge to certain individuals and does not give it to all, that is not because of the Master's incapacity to give to all, but because of the incapacity of one and all to receive Knowledge. The latter incapacity is due to the lack of a sufficiently deep and strong connection with the Master or for want of complete surrender to his will, or on account of the absence of the required degree of preparedness on the part of the individuals concerned.

Under these circumstances, it would be like throwing pearls before swine for the Master to offer Knowledge to one and all irrespective of the individual's receptivity. The fact is that scores of Masters have come without beginning and scores of Masters will come without end, and still it would be quite true to say that there is no question of any time at all in spite of the countless epochs involved. If Knowledge cannot come within the purview of one's imagination, how can one be able to imagine the One possessing Knowledge?

On one side, Knowledge is so very, very small that it may be likened to a mustard seed; and on the other, it contains and covers everything in existence, including the "nothing" or "ignorance of Maya." This *Dnyan,* which in Sufism is termed *Marefat,* lies in the certainty of "becoming." There are three stages of this certainty. First is the certainty by intellectual conviction called *Illmul-Yakeen.* Second is the certainty of *Anicol-Yakeen* through actual "Seeing"; and the third, the certainty of certainties, is by "Becoming" or *Hukkal-Yakeen.*

What the Vedantists say about our being one with God,—even that is not the intellectual conviction of *Illmul-Yakeen,* because when we hear that we are one with God, we imagine only what the intellect grasps temporarily. The temporary understanding can check the conviction, and nothing can upset the holder of that conviction, and when one actually begins to see what one has grasped permanently, then the *Yakeen* or certainty of conviction can be said to be spiritually firm for all time. It is only after one becomes united with what one IS that the certainty of conviction is *Dnyan* or *Hakul-Yakeen.*

Now, you all are ordinary men. This knowledge of manhood on your part does not depend upon intellect or reasoning whatsoever. You just know that you are men. None of you ever thinks, "I am a man, I am stone," etc. That is because your knowledge that you are men is self-knowledge of your manhood, and is not the outcome of a mere belief based on what you hear about the feelings and experience of others. Similarly, when you actually feel and find that you have become God, you are then really God; and this "becoming" is the Knowledge which the Master can and does impart at the right moment in literally no time at all.

True *mahatmas* and *walis* can and may give the shadow of Knowledge to anyone by influencing, through a touch, sound or sight, the centers and seats of knowledge; but even that shadow may be enough to make one lose one's physical body.

We all are, in a way, hypocrites, inasmuch as we always try to justify ourselves, right or wrong. According to the Vedantists and the Sufis, God does everything; everything is done according to His Will and in accordance with His laws. In a way, that is all right; but being short of one truth, the whole of it is not right. And the lack of truth is the lack of experience behind the assertions. Without having gained the actual experience, to act according to facts of experience is not only silly like a tutored parrot expressing love to a girl, but such assertions based on mere reasoning and logic lead to lust and dust. The reactions of the actions based on such "ignorance of knowledge" are too terrible to contemplate, apart from other consequences like lunacy or nervous breakdown.

Bhakti-marg, which is the sum and substance of every religion, makes us frigidly rigid over "right is right" and "wrong is wrong," leading to a dry-as-dust, brittle and boring attitude of the mind. Under yoga practices, the experiencing of different kinds of temporary *samadhis* brings forgetfulness of Reality and causes the yogi to lose sight of the Goal itself. By *"jap-tap"* and *"chilla-kashi"* he is entrapped in novel, but nonetheless limited, powers that eventually prove a boomerang for his mind.

The real "headache" lies in the fact that we really have to become what we really are, and therefore in order to gain God, we must first lose Him. Suppose I am God; then first I have to lose myself in order to be able to find myself.

Complete loss of God means, wants are not there, desires are not there, likes or dislikes are not there, you are not there, God is not there; in short, nothing is there: and this is Real *Fana* or the Divine Vacuum. The moment this *Fana* takes place, at that very moment, God comes into His own full glory of the everlasting *Baqa*. This is not according to the Western conception of Realization of "this inside" or "that outside" but is discovery of God, by God, for God.

Even when God is lost and found, the life of God is not there. The life of God can be led by regaining ordinary human sobriety and, at the same time, retaining one's Divinity Individualized. For example, Sai Baba's* Individuality is eternal, although his work in the different planes and spheres of existence is no longer there. Only those who were then in the respective planes of consciousness know about Sai Baba's work in those particular planes; and all the work of Sai Baba in all the planes at

---

* The Perfect Master, Sai Baba of Shirdi

one and the same time was known only to him and his contemporaries.

Mind Must Go

Mind is never transformed. Ego is transformed only once.*

Today you feel that you are a man, tomorrow you die and then when you are born again your mental impressions give you the feeling that you are a woman; all this is false. Mind's attitude is changed according to circumstances, but mind remains mind, whether it is uplifted or depressed. Mind can be happy and it can be miserable. It is the attitude of the mind which thus changes. Mind creates worlds, delusions, illusions, etc., but mind remains as mind. Mind cannot be transformed. Why? Because it is *not* one in itself. Mind survives by desires and thoughts and it is made up of impressions. Ego is one in itself but this Ego (the real "I") is now bound by this mind. And this mind which is made up of false impressions makes the real "I" think itself false. Mind makes you think of birth, death, happiness, miseries, etc., as real things, but nothing can be more false than this.

You are now here alive in the body, in your senses. Have you any impression of how you were born, how your birth took place? No . . . because you were not born at all. It is the mind that gives you the impression that you are here, or there, and so on. It is the mind that gives you the impressions which make you say, "She is my wife" or "He is my husband," etc. Mind keeps us continually "tap dancing." If you knew that your wife, child, etc., are one, if you knew that you never die, never suffer, etc., you would know you are all-in-all. But the mind is there to baffle you. Mind says "Beware! She is your wife, they are your children, etc." *Mind creates these false impressions and makes the real "I" think itself false.* To think "I am body, I am young, old, I am a man, a woman, I am this or that" are all impressions created by the mind.

Mind might make one say "I am God," but cannot

* By Ego is meant *"Astistv"*—"I."

make itself *feel* "I am God." So long as mind is there, Ego cannot be transformed from its false attitude to its real state. Mind thus also makes you say that you are infinite, all-powerful, and so forth, but you do not experience it. Why? Because mind, which is made up of false impressions makes you—the real "I"—feel yourself as the small limited "i." If the false ego is to have the experience of its real, original state, the mind must go. As long as the mind is there, even though its outlook may undergo a change, the real "I am God" state cannot be experienced. In sound sleep, mind has temporarily ceased; but ego is there. The impressions again make the mind wake up, and the mind again makes the ego feel false. In innumerable lives and forms, the ego is there. The mind is there also, but the mind's impressions change and so accordingly the body changes, and then its experiences also undergo changes. Therefore, for the false "I" to become real "I," *mind must go.*

This grip of the mind has bound us so tight that the more we try to escape, the more we find ourselves bound, because mind has to be destroyed from its root. But who is going to destroy it? Mind has to destroy itself. Yet that is an impossible task. The very process of destroying itself creates impressions in the mind of this effort at self-destruction, and so one gets more bound. Says Hafiz: "You yourself are the veil, oh Hafiz! And so remove thyself." Now how to remove yourself? The very process of removing creates fresh *sanskaras* (impressions).

There is a story of four Iranis who heard about how the soul leaves the body and how it goes to the sky, etc. One day, being intoxicated with *bhang,** they caught hold of a wheel of a cart and went on pulling at it for a long time, thinking that thus they would be able to detach their souls, but obviously this didn't help and they realized that they had injured themselves in the bargain. There have been many attempts of this type to destroy the mind, which is made up of impressions of every kind—good, bad, low, high, etc. Thousands have thought of destroying the mind—through the main paths of Action, Meditation, Knowledge and Love. These have been

* A native beverage.

38

chalked out by the Masters for the purpose of destroying the mind while still retaining consciousness.

Let us consider how, through the Path of Action, the goal of *Man-O-Nash,* that annihilation of the mind which transforms the false "I" into the real "I," can be attained. Perfect Masters saw that actions which have false ego and impressionful mind as their background feed the mind instead of destroying it. They saw that everyone has to do actions; even the laziest of men has to eat, drink, etc. These actions, instead of destroying the mind, only feed it again. Therefore they conceived of "action-less action." That means to act but in such a way that the effect is as if no action were done. In this way, past impressions of actions get spent up mentally through experience of happiness and misery, but no new impressions are created.

Suppose you help someone without any thought of self-interest; suppose you try to protect a woman and in doing so, get beaten and the police arrest you and put you in jail. These happenings spend up some of your past *sanskaras,* but as you had no self-interest, no fresh *sanskaras* are formed. This process is so long and complicated that one can attain *Man-O-Nash* through action only after many *Yugas.**

The real goal of life is not the death of the ego but the death of the mind. So when Mohammed or Zoroaster or Jesus talked of being born once, or dying once, they meant the death of the mind. Mind is born from the very beginning—even before the stone age. This birth takes place only once and the death of mind also takes place only once. When the mind dies, the false ego is transformed into Reality. Real ego is never born and it never dies. Ego is always real, but due to the mind, the ego feels and acts as the limited and false "I."

Now mind goes on taking bodies according to its good or bad impressions. This taking and shedding bodies is not the death of either the mind or the ego. After the physical death, the mind remains, with all its accumulated impressions. It is the impressions which make the mind take bodies so that the impressions might be experienced in the process of being wiped out, while

* Cycles of time.

the ego remains a witness. Even when you are fast asleep, the ego and the mind are still there. The impressions wake you up so that they might be experienced and in the process get wiped out. This phenomena is also in a way the daily birth of the body. When one body is dropped, another comes up; although there is a certain time lag between the giving up of one body and the taking on of another. In between, there are the mind-states of heaven, hell, etc. The mind has to die *in* this body; thus the Masters have chalked out different ways to attain this *Man-O-Nash* or annihilation of the mind during life.

As long as the mind is there the body is also there and there is continuous action. Only when the mind is at rest, completely stilled or unconscious, does action stop ninety-nine per cent. Even then the one per cent of actions continue, such as breathing, snoring, turning in bed, etc. Thus actions continue and there is no escape from them. Actions create impressions which again feed the mind, and so there is no remedy or way for the ego to rid itself of impressions and experience its Real State. So the Masters suggested action to kill action, that is, action done in such a way that the effect of the action is impotent, i.e., it creates no result which leads to any kind of binding. For example: a scorpion by nature wags its tail and stings anyone who comes near it. Now suppose the dangerous sting is removed, even then the scorpion goes on wagging its tail and continues to behave as before; but the action is rendered impotent, without dangerous results—that is, the bad effect of the action is removed. If actions have to be without binding, their effects which lead to binding have to be eliminated.

The world and its activities are really worthless. Actions continue whether they are good or bad, and therefore the Masters have said, "Act in such a way that the actions do not bind you and impressions are not created." This is an almost impossible task, as explained below. Yet there are three ways by which action can be done without creating the impressions and the consequent bindings:

1) To act, but with absolutely no thought that you are acting. This must be a continuous process. The ego must not give even one moment for the mind to exert its

influence. In fact, you act for others and not for yourself. This selfless action, which is also called selfless service, or Karma Yoga, is also almost impossible, because the moment you think, "I am serving others, I must help, I must uplift a certain cause," you are caught. For a leader it is very risky unless this thought about himself is given up 100 per cent continuously. This point may be explained further. If a leader asks others to sacrifice everything for some cause, with the best of motives and with no self-interest, but fails to give up every thought of self 100 per cent continuously, then the result is a disaster. All the *Sanskaras* (impressions) of the whole group fall on him and even his followers are caught up in the impressions, even though they might have acted with the best of intentions. A similar disaster occurs in case of a guru and disciple, if there is any thought of self on either side. Even pity for others should not be there. In short, when action has to be without effect then it must be done without self-interest, which is almost impossible.

2) The second way is that whatever good or bad you do, you dedicate to God or your Master. This, too, is almost impossible as the dedication has to be continuous without a moment's break. If you are able to do so, then impressions are not created by your actions; but if there is a break even once, the reaction is disastrous and all the *sanskaras* fall upon you.

3) The third way is to do whatever you are asked to do by a Master who is free from impressions and whose mind is destroyed. Such actions do not bind you. This, too, is difficult. You must have 100 per cent unflinching faith in the Master; even a moment's doubt is fatal. Krishna had to convince Arjuna that He was in everyone and that no one died, as all were dead already. Then what Arjuna did was "action without action."

The above three ways are thus almost impossible to attain. So how should one act? To be involved in the mere *"sansar"* [worldly matters] with your wife, children, and to act results in your getting bound with hoops of iron. But submissive, loose and weak impressions are created by actions done without self-interest, even if at times thoughts of helping or pitying others come into the mind, because mind's part is to make the ego identify with the body and not feel false, and to experience the *sanskaras*. But when the mind sees that the ego is not so ready to accept its dictatorship, then the impressions formed by the actions of the above type are weak. Such actions are therefore eventually of help towards attaining *Man-O-Nash*.

When Knowledge comes, it comes in a flash; God-hood is what you then experience. God is Knowledge, and in a moment you know everything and then you know that there was nothing to know.

Some Masters have chalked out ways of destroying the mind through mind itself, by means of meditation and concentration; when mind is concentrated, its further function is weakened and the impressions exhaust themselves. But in this process of meditation and concentration, *Man-O-Nash* is almost impossible, because mind has the habit of getting its impressions carried out; when the mind feels frustrated, it gets more desperate. The moment you sit for meditation, thoughts which you never got before sometimes come to you, and eventually one of the following three things happen: (1) you get fed up because you cannot concentrate, (2) you get sleepy or drowsy, or (3) more bad thoughts enter your mind and you have to give up your attempts.

But if you have a brave heart and you patiently persist, then, in a very few cases, the mind is temporarily stilled.

Now this results in one of two things—one goes into a state of trance or one gets a sort of *Samadhi*. Neither this trance *(Hal)* nor *Samadhi* are *Man-O-Nash*. Such a *Samadhi* becomes a profession in some cases; and trance becomes like dope and one gets addicted to it. One enjoys that trance, but it is temporary. There have been cases of those going into *Samadhi* and while coming down, getting as their first thought the same thought they had while going up into the *Samadhi*. Thus, if they had the thought of money before entering into *Samadhi,* they get the same thought when coming out of it.

Some Masters have taught that the best way to achieve *Man-O-Nash* is to forget oneself through devotion and to give the mind no chance of having new impressions. The question is how to forget oneself through devotion *(Bhakti Marg)*. When one is devoted 100 per cent, then one forgets oneself. But this, too, is practically impossible, because such devotion and forgetfulness have to be continuous. Hafiz has said, "If you want the presence of the Beloved, do not absent yourself from the memory of the Beloved." You must not be for one moment without this devotion or without self-forgetfulness, when is almost an impossibility. Therefore one Master has said, "One moment with the Perfect Master is better than a hundred years of sincere prayers."

Now some Masters have taught that mind must be diverted if it is to be killed. Mind makes the ego say "I am body." Thefore make the mind say, "I am not body, I am not this and not that, I am God." Now this, too, is almost impossible, because mind has its own impressions and to compel this mind to say what it thinks to be false and contrary to its own impressions seems like an hypocritical act. For example, mind knows that it is Mr. So and So. Now, if this person's mind says, "I am not a human being, but I am God," then at that very moment the mind thinks that is lying. The result is that this tires out the heart —the emotions and love; the mind cannot accomplish actionless actions because mind says, "I am God, what do I have to act for?" Mind says, mind cannot forget itself in devotion because it repeats, "I am God, to whom should I pray?"

So *Man-O-Nash* becomes impossible. But if selfless action (even if not perfect) is persisted in, a stage is reached when mind is permanently at peace. It sees God, but it is not yet destroyed. If through *Bhakti* a state of love is achieved by which constant devotion is attained, then this peace of mind and seeing of God comes. So if one says, "I am God, I am not body," and persists in this saying with 100 per cent faithfulness at the cost of everything, then this peace of mind is achieved. But for *Man-O-Nash* there is always the need of help of the Perfect Master. One who is free from the binding of impressions can "uproot" the minds of others, even of masses.

In short, there are all these ways to attempt *Man-O-Nash* and to make one feel superficially "I am God, Infinite, Eternal, etc." But it is rightly said, "You cannot step out of your nature, so how can you aspire to enter the threshold of your Beloved?"

Following different paths, different people encounter different difficulties. Some who do not know the technique of meditation go mad. Some say that they should never see a woman. They get so nervous about it all.

The fact is all is God, but you are misled by this shameless mind. The mind is so shameless that the more you wish to get rid of it, the more you get entangled in it, just as when you try to take out one foot from the mire, your other foot gets stuck more deeply. All the same you have to get rid of this troublesome mind.

Man-O-Nash is real *Samadhi* for the mind. The mind is uprooted and this is the death of mind; the ego immediately feels, "I am everything," and it is disassociated from all experiences of the body, for it has now no concern with the body. At this moment either the shock is too strong and the body falls, or the momentum keeps the body going for some time and then it falls.

Man-O-Nash or
The Annihilation of the Mind

> GOD *is everywhere and does everything.*
> GOD *is within us and knows everything.*
> GOD *is without us and sees everything.*
> GOD *is beyond us and IS everything.*

The One All-pervading, All-comprehending, All-powerful God, who is the Self of our selves, and besides whom nothing is real, has helped me and guided me during the *Man-O-Nash* period of my work,* and now makes me dictate to you the following:

To try to understand with the mind that which the mind can never understand, is futile; and to try to express by sounds of language and in form of words the transcendental state of the soul, is even more futile. All that can be said, and has been said, and will be said, by those who live and experience that state, is that when the false self is lost, the Real Self is found; that the birth of the Real can

* 1951

only follow the death of the false; and that dying to ourselves . . . the true death which ends all dying . . . is the only way to perpetual life. This means that when the mind with its satellites . . . desires, cravings, longings . . . is completely consumed by the fire of Divine Love, then the infinite, indestructible, indivisible, eternal Self is manifested. This is *Man-O-Nash,* the annihilation of the false, limited, miserable, ignorant, destructible "I," to be replaced by the real "I"; the eternal possessor of Infinite Knowledge, Love, Power, Peace, Bliss and Glory, in its unchangeable existence. *Man-O-Nash* is bound to result in this glorious state in which plurality goes and Unity comes, ignorance goes and Knowledge comes, binding goes and Freedom comes. We are all permanently lodged in this shoreless Ocean of infinite Knowledge, and yet are infinitely ignorant of it until the mind . . . which is the source of this ignorance . . . vanishes forever; for ignorance ceases to exist when the mind ceases to exist.

Unless and until ignorance is removed and Knowledge is gained . . . the Knowledge whereby the Divine Life is experienced and lived . . . everything pertaining to the spiritual seems paradoxical.

God, whom we do not see, we say is real; and the world, which we do see, we say is false. In experience, what exists for us does not really exist; and what does not exist for us, really exists.

We must lose ourselves in order to find ourselves: thus loss itself is gain.

We must die to self to live in God: thus death means Life.

We must become completely void inside to be completely possessed by God: thus complete emptiness means absolute Fullness.

We must become naked of selfhood by possessing nothing, so as to be absorbed in the infinity of God: thus nothing means Everything.

Bhakti Yoga

Out of a number of practices which lead to the ultimate goal of humanity—God-Realization—Bhakti Yoga is one of the most important. Almost the whole of humanity is concerned with Bhakti Yoga, which, in simple words, means the art of worship. But it must be understood in all its true aspects, and not merely in a narrow and shallow sense, in which the term is commonly used and interpreted.

The profound worship based on the high ideals of philosophy and spirituality, prompted by divine love, doubtless constitutes true Bhakti Yoga. It follows then that the various ceremonies and rituals, which are part and parcel of every creed or the *shariat** of every religion, constitute only its shadow. Nevertheless, it may be said that the ritualistic worship, which the masses of humanity confuse with religion, is Bhakti Yoga in its incipient or initial stage. A number of the ceremonies performed by the followers of every creed are doubtless useless, but those ceremonies and modes of offering prayers, which are essentially based on the principle of conveying or evoking worship, may be said to constitute elementary Bhakti Yoga.

Although Bhakti Yoga cannot be divided into separate, watertight compartments, it may be said to have three principal stages. The first stage, which is elementary, concerns itself with ritualistic worship. The *Namaz* of the Muslims, the *Tal-Bhajan* and the *Sandhya-Pujas* of the Hindus, the *Kusti* and *Bhantars* of the Zoroastrians, the prayers of the Christians, etc., are no doubt Bhakti-worship in rudimentary stages. The first stage of Bhakti Yoga is therefore general, and almost everyone is concerned with it and can practice it.

The second stage, which is intermediate, concerns itself with the constant remembrance of God. The worshipper, through constant mental or physical repetitions (*Nam-Smaran* or *Zikra*) of any one name of God, achieves the fixity of thought on God, without the medium of any ceremony. In other words, when a person's thoughts are always directed towards God, throughout the waking state, even while eating or talking, he may be said to be in the second stage of Bhakti Yoga.

This kind of constant remembrance of God must not be confounded with meditation. In meditation, one

---

* Ceremonial side of religion

makes an attempt to achieve fixity of thought; whereas one who has reached the second stage of Bhakti Yoga already possesses the one sole and single thought for God, and therefore has no more need of organized thinking. Just as a variety of thoughts come to an ordinary man, even without the intention on his part to have them, the Bhakti yogi in the second stage simply cannot help thinking about the Lord, wherever and however he may be. This fixity of thought on God is higher Bhakti or worship.

The third stage, which is advanced, concerns itself with divine love and longing of a high order. The higher Bhakti of the second stage ultimately leads the aspirant to this third or highest stage of Bhakti Yoga; in other words, to the highest Bhakti and to the true love. The one in this stage can be called the true lover of God. For him there is no question of fixity of thought. He is beyond thought. His thoughts, so to say, have got melted into the blazing and all-consuming fire of an intense longing for the Beloved—God. So much so, that far from thinking about his physical needs, the aspirant in this stage of Bhakti or love, is almost incognizant of his very corporality.

From this survey of the three stages of Bhakti Yoga, it is quite evident that for householders, men of busy avocations, in short, for the masses, the practice of worship is possible only up to the first stage. The average man should follow his creed, whatever it may be, in all sincerity, regardless of the rewards to come, and with the only aim and object of—"I want nothing but You —God."

But when I say "following one's own creed," I mean that everybody should be free to base his worship on the religious ideas and methods that appeal to him most, and not that one should stop dead at believing or disbelieving certain statements of a particular scripture, about subjects that are generally beyond the sphere of intellect. It is the act of worship from the heart, and not thoughts and beliefs, that counts in the religious province.

Thus, for a Hindu, a Muslim, a Christian, a Parsi, the best Bhakti is the performance of the *Puja,* the *Namaz,* the prayers, and the *Kusti* ceremony, respectively. But the performance must be from the very depths of the heart, and with the only object of "I want nothing but

You (God)." Otherwise, a religion, however beautiful be its teachings, however grand be its philosophy, becomes nothing but a mere farce, which people indulge in generally more through force of habit and fear of society than through any idea of true devotion and worship.

Unless there is the will to worship, no number of ceremonies and no amount of lip-prayer will ever serve the true purpose of religion. It is one thing to learn by heart the whole of a scripture; it is quite another thing to repeat a single sentence of it from the heart. A Hindu may have the *Shastras* at his fingertips, but if he lacks in devotion from the heart, he is no better than a typewriter or a calculating machine.

A Muslim may laugh at so-called idol-worship; but he becomes guilty of stray-thought worship, if, while placing his forehead down in a *Sijda** in the course of his *Namaz,* without being prompted by the will to worship, he is attacked by objectionable thoughts, for it means that he is at that time paying homage, not to the Almighty, but to those very thoughts. For instance, if a Muslim gets the thought of any man or woman, while doing the *Sijda,* it amounts to having offered the *Sijda* to that man or woman, and thus the *Namaz* turns into a farce.

This point was convincingly elucidated by the Muslim saint, Sufi-Sarmast (who was averse to offering ritualistic prayers) when King Aurangzeb once forced him to participate in the congregational *Namaz*. The Saint joined the congregation against his will, but he soon revolted against it by calling loudly to the Imam, who, at the particular moment of leading the prayers, was mentally busy arranging the finances for the forthcoming marriage of his daughter, that "the God of the Imam was beneath his feet." The Saint's words were verified later when a treasure-trove was actually found just beneath the spot where Sufi-Samrmast was standing at the time of praying with the congregation.

To sum up, it is possible for everyone, belonging to any creed and to any station in life, to practice Bhakti Yoga or the true art of worship in its first stage. The act of worship should spring from the heart. Let it be borne in mind that worship from the heart presupposes great

* prostration

THE PATH OF LOVE

efforts. It cannot be evoked with a mere wish. If one decides upon practicing true Bhakti, one has to make heroic efforts in order to achieve fixity of mind, for contrary thoughts are very likely to disturb one's mind. It is because the average person's frame of mind is averse to remaining unchanged for any considerable period of time, that the repeated efforts to evoke deep devotion are essential; and in fact are the turning point in such practices that distinguish the right sense of religion from the shallow show of a mere routine.

Some persons may be so constituted that they can readily take to the second stage of Bhakti Yoga, without having passed through the first stage. But whether the devotee has or has not passed through the first stage, in the beginning of the second stage, he has to make vigorous efforts in thinking about the Almighty as much and as often as possible. The efforts must be continued until he becomes above efforts; and he becomes above efforts only when worship from the heart becomes his second nature. He who can naturally worship from the heart without finding it necessary to make artificial efforts, may justifiably be said to have attained to higher Bhakti.

Let it be noted that it is not necessary for a man to stop carrying out his worldly duties and obligations, to achieve or to practice this higher Bhakti. He may conduct his business or follow his profession, he may lead the family life and look after all his necessary external requirements; but amidst all his worldly engagements he should ever be alert on the Lord. The more he can remember the object of the heart-worship, along with the routine work of his everyday life, the better for him. Besides reiterating the name of the Almighty in the ordinary manner, the seeker of the subjective, spiritual sidelights in the second, more advanced stage of Bhakti Yoga should make it a rule to retire into a dark room all alone for about a couple of hours every night. During this period of retirement he must try to avoid all thoughts save that of "I want You, O Lord," and repeat continuously any one of the names of the Almighty which he has adopted for the purpose of *Nam-Smaran*.

This is the best course open for those who neither feel satisfied with objective worship, nor can afford to renounce all for God. If sincerely followed, this intermediate practice is bound to bear fruit sooner or later and provide the aspirant with the subjective "glimpses" of the great Reality in some way or another. For instance, one may be able to see or hear without using the gross organs of sight and sound; or perhaps even get established on the Path itself.

But for the few who insist, from the very depth of their souls and from the innermost core of their heart, on seeing the Reality actually face to face, at all costs and consequences, there is but one way. And that is complete renunciation. Such heroes must not only possess the indomitable courage of renouncing the world, forsaking all possessions and properties, tearing up all external connections, but also of practicing internal renunciation, which means giving up all desires and passions, but entertaining the aspiration for God-realization.

After renouncing fully and faithfully, both in the letter and spirit of the word, as described above, the hero-aspirant must either surrender himself completely to a Perfect Master, in whom he has faith; or retire for good in a forest, or on a mountain, or along the riverside, with the name of the Lord on his lips, with the thought of God in his mind, with the aspiration of seeing Him in his heart. In short, until the aspirant comes to the goal, or the guide—a living Perfect Master,—he should lead the life of renunciation, wandering or sitting in solitude, ever ready to lay down his life in the cause of his aspiration. But this does not mean he should never feel hungry or wherever or whenever food is available he should avoid it. Renunciation certainly means that one should, among other things, cease to think about food. But hunger is not always the result of thinking. One never requires thought about hunger in order to become hungry. It is as natural as breathing. However, it has great connection with the intensity of Bhakti or longing on the part of the aspirant. The more intense becomes the divine longing, the more reduced become the physical needs.

Even on this phenomenal plane, we often find worldly people becoming indifferent for a long time to what we call the indispensable necessities of life, in the heat and attraction of an absorbing work and pleasure.

This is just what happens on the spiritual plane too. One may become so very preoccupied with the ideal in view as to forget all about these supposedly indispensable necessities of life for months together, without permanently harming oneself physically. No harm can come where there is no thought of any harm. And when we say that those who really insist on seeing God must renounce all and go about with their very lives in their shirt sleeves, we certainly mean that no consideration for any personal loss or danger should be entertained. We do not mean that the aspirant should commit suicide; but he should certainly cease to cling to life and be prepared to lose it if and when circumstances demand it.

This may seem impracticable, and it is certainly next to impossible for most persons to reach this height of Bhakti Yoga. Yet every human being is potentially capable of demonstrating this high achievement; and some, though very few in number, do manifest divinity in this way from time to time.

To give a recent example, His Holiness Sadguru Upasni Maharaj of Sakori seated himself in seclusion about forty-five years ago on a hill near Nasik, for fully one year continuously, and during this whole period took neither food nor water, even once. And yet he remained alive! A God-realized person can, if he or she so wishes, remain without food, water, or even breathing, for years together, but there is no wonder about it, as the God-Realized One possesses infinite powers.

But in the above example the noteworthy point is that at the time of remaining without food or water for one year, Shri Upasni Maharaj was not God-Realized. It was simply owing to the intensity of his divine longing that Shri Maharaj was able to forget the consciousness and needs of his corporeal frame.

The question may be asked as to what a man, who is completely renounced and retired into solitude, should do to secure the bare necessities of life, i.e., food, when he feels a great pinch of hunger. He must go a-begging for food, and for this purpose, may mix slightly with others temporarily. But he must be prepared to partake of and be satisfied with any kind of food, whether it is agreeable or disagreeable, and sufficient or insufficient.

And no sooner is his most acute need supplied, than he should go back and remain in solitude all by himself, with the thought of God.

It should not be implied from the above that begging, as practiced by a large number of so-called *Sadhus* and other professional beggars, who are a curse to society and a disgrace to spirituality, is here advocated or condoned. On the contrary, it is a fact that the first and foremost law of spirituality and God-finding is to *give,* from the start to the finish. And the true renouncer, the great hero who has given up all desires—the root cause of beggary—when he begs for and takes food and bare necessities from a man of the world, he gives that man an opportunity to serve and share in the great and noble search for God. In order to elucidate the point we will now discuss *Sahkam* and *Nishkam,* the two kinds of Bhakti.

A worship may be sincere, it may be from the heart, but if the worshipper offers it with the expectation of any return, whether in the shape of worldly benefits, or for blessings in the life hereafter, his worship is *Sahkam.* And this *Sahkam* is generally connected with the first stage of Bhakti Yoga. When worship from the heart is offered for the sake of worship only, and without any thoughts of reward in this life or the next, it is called *Nishkam,* and is concerned with the second and the third stage of Bhakti Yoga. True, the aspiration to see and be one with God is the chief motive of the highest worship, but this aspiration is poles asunder from worldly desires. This aspiration is such that even when one comes face to face with God, it remains in full blaze until the Union is effected—as evident from what Hafiz exclaimed when he reached the sixth plane, *viz.*:

> *"Khatiram vakhti havas kardi kay binam chizha Ta toora didam na kardi jooz ba didarat haves!"*
>
> *"I always desired to see different things, but since I have seen You, I desire to see nothing but You."*

Efforts may be made to turn *Sahkam Bhakti* into *Nishkam Bhakti* even in the first stage. In the beginning worship is necessarily *Sakham.* A man may cease to worship God for the sake of temporal gains. But it seldom happens that, while worshipping, a man in the initial stage can help avoiding thoughts for reward in the life to come. And although this *Sahkam Bhakti* is nothing but beggary, it is all the same the beginning of true Bhakti, for, while begging directly or indirectly of God for any kind of favors, the worshipper sincerely praises God. Because the praise, actuated by the thoughts of gain, is from the heart, it is likely to turn into disinterested praise, which in turn leads to *Nishkam Bhakti*.

Love and God-Love

Of all the forces that can best overcome all difficulties, is the force of love, because the greatest Law of God is Love, which holds the key to all problems. This mighty force not only enables one to put the ideal of selfless service into practice, but also transforms one into God. It has been possible through love for man to become God; and when God becomes man, it is also due to His Love for His beings.

Love is dynamic in action and contagious in effect. Pure love is matchless in majesty; it has no parallel in power and there is no darkness it cannot dispel. It is the undying flame that has set life aglow. The lasting emancipation of man depends upon his love for God and upon God's love for one and all.

Where there is love, there is Oneness and, in complete Oneness, the Infinite is realized completely at all times and in every sphere of life, be it science, art, religion, or beauty. The spirit of true love and sacrifice is beyond all ledgers and needs no measures. A constant wish to love and be loving and a non-calculating will to sacrifice in every walk of life, high and low, big and small, between home and office, streets and cities, countries and continents are the best anti-selfish measures that man can take in order to be really self-ful and joyful.

Love also means suffering and pain for oneself and happiness for others. To the giver, it is suffering without malice or hatred. To the receiver, it is a blessing without obligation. Love alone knows how to give without necessarily bargaining for a return. There is nothing that love cannot achieve and there is nothing that love cannot sacrifice.

Love for God, love for fellow-beings, love for service and love of sacrifices; in short, love in any shape and form is the finest "give and take" in the world. Ultimately, it is love that will bring about the much-desired universal leveling of human beings all over the world, without necessarily disturbing the inherent diversities of details about mankind.

All the same, in order to burst out in a mighty big spirit to serve as a beacon for those who may yet be groping in the darkness of selfishness, love needs to be kindled and rekindled in the abysmal darkness of selfish thoughts, selfish words and selfish deeds.

The light of love is not free from its fire of sacrifice. Like heat and light, love and sacrifice go hand in hand. The true spirit of sacrifice that springs spontaneously does not and cannot reserve itself for particular objects and special occasions. Love and coercion can never go together. Love has to spring spontaneously from within. It is in no way amenable to any form of inner or outer force and it cannot be forced upon anybody, yet it can be awakened in one through love itself.

Love cannot be born of mere determination; through the exercise of will, one can at best be dutiful. One may, through struggle and effort, succeed in securing that his external action is in conformity with his conception of what is right; but such action is spiritually barren because it lacks the inward duty of spontaneous love.

Like every great virtue, love, the mainspring of all life, can also be misapplied. It may lead to the height of God-intoxication or to the depths of despair. No better example can be given of the two polarities of love and their effects than that of Mary Magdalene before and after meeting Jesus.

Between these two extremes are many kinds of love. On the one hand, love does exist in all the phases of human life; but here it is latent or is limited and poisoned by personal ambitions, racial pride, narrow loyalties and rivalries and by attachment to sex, nationality, sect, caste, or religion. On the other hand, pure and real love has also its stages, the highest being the gift of God to love Him. When one truly loves God, one longs for union with Him, and this supreme longing is based on the desire of giving up one's whole being to the beloved.

True love is very different from an evanescent outburst of indulgent emotionalism or the enervating stupor of a slumbering heart. It can never come to those whose heart is darkened by selfish cravings or weakened by constant reliance upon the lures and stimulations of the passing objects of sense.

Even when one truly loves humanity, one longs to give one's all for its happiness. When one truly loves one's country, there is the longing to sacrifice one's very life without seeking reward and without the least thought of having loved and served. When one truly loves one's friends, there is the longing to help them without making them feel under the least obligation. When truly loving one's enemies, one longs to make them friends. True love for one's parents or family makes one long to give them every comfort at the cost of one's own. Thought of self is always absent in the different longings connected with the various stages of pure, real love; a single thought of self would be an adulteration.

Divine Love is qualitatively different from human love. Human love is for the *many in the one* and Divine Love is for the *One in the many*. Human love leads to innumerable complications and tangles; but Divine Love leads to integration and freedom. Human love in its personal and impersonal aspects is limited; but Divine Love, with its fusion of the personal and the impersonal aspects, is Infinite in being and expression. Divine Love makes us be true to ourselves and to others and makes us live truly and honestly. Thus, it is the solution to all our difficulties and problems; it frees us from every kind of binding; purifies our hearts and glorifies our being.

To those whose hearts are pure and simple, true love comes as a gift through the activating grace of a Perfect Master, and this Divine Love will perform the supreme miracle of bringing God into the hearts of men. All the same, human love should not be despised, even when it is fraught with limitations. It is bound to break through all these limitations and initiate an aspirant in the eternal life in the Truth.

God does not listen to the language of the tongue which constitutes *Japs* (mental repetitions), *Mantras* (verbal repetitions), *Zikra* (either kind of repetition), and devotional songs. He does not listen to the language of the mind which constitutes meditation, concentration and thoughts about God. He listens only to the language of the heart, which constitutes love. The most practical way for the common man to express this language of the heart, whilst attending to daily-life duties, is to speak lovingly, think lovingly, and act lovingly towards all mankind, irrespective of caste, creed and position, taking God to be present in each and every one.

To realize God, we must love Him, losing ourselves in His Infinite Self. We can love God by surrendering to the Perfect Master who is God's personal Manifestation. We can also love God by loving our fellow-beings, by giving them happiness at the cost of our own happiness, by rendering them service at sacrifice of our interests and by dedicating our lives at the altar of selfless work. When we love God intensely through any of these channels, we finally know Him to be our own Self.

The beginning of real love is obedience, and the highest aspect of this love which surpasses that of love itself is the aspect which culminates into the perfect obedience or supreme resignation to the Will and Wish of the Beloved. In this love are embodied all Yogas known to saints and seekers.

The Aura and the Halo

An aura and a halo are two different things and people are unable to distinguish between the two. Few people know that an aura and a halo are quite different in their respective natures, despite their close interconnection. No man can ever possess both aura and halo completely developed at one and the same time.

Like their respective shadows, every man, woman, child and baby has an aura, but only a very few individuals have a halo on the varying phases of its development; and fewer still possess a full halo. An aura is the reflection of the emotions of an individual mind, just as any physical thing possesses its shadow on the physical plane. The

TABLE: THE AURA AND THE HALO

By Meher Baba

INDIVIDUAL	PLANE	NATURE	AURA OF 7 COLORS			HALO OF LIGHT	SPIRITUAL BENEFIT	
			Number of Colors More or Less Prominent	Number of Colors Almost Faint	Materialistic Influence		Indirect*	Direct**
Ordinary	Gross	False Illusion	7	Nil	100%	Nil	Nil	Nil
Advanced	1st Subtle	Beginning of Real Illusion	6	1	80%	Faint	5%	Nil
More Advanced	2nd Subtle	Real Illusion	5	2	65%	Dim	7%	Nil
Most Advanced	3rd Subtle	Real Illusion (High)	4	3	55%	Fair	10%	Nil
Dangling	4th—Junction of Subtle and Mental	Dangerous	2 (Very Bright Red and Blue)	5	50%	Unsteady	50%***	Nil
Illumined	5th Mental	Real Illusion (Higher)	3	4	30%	Bright	25%	25%
Most Illumined	6th Mental	Real Illusion (Highest)	2 (Blue and Pink)	5	15%	Very Bright	50%	50%
God-Realized	7th Reality	Real	Nil	Nil	Nil	Nil	100%	Nil
Perfect Master	7th Perfection (Reality plus one and all planes)	Real	Nil	Nil	100%	Most Bright	100%	100%

* According to the efforts of a Seeker.
** Given consciously with full force.
*** 50% possibility of harm instead of benefit.

†Note: Percentages shown above are not actual, but symbolic of proportions in ordinary terms.

halo begins to *appear* when the aura begins to *disappear.*

The difference between an aura—the mental reflection—and any physical shadow is tremendous. Shadows depend upon their physical forms, but an individual aura remains unaffected, even when the person concerned drops his physical body, because in spite of physical death, the individual continues to possess both a mind and the impressions in it, as well as a subtle body, which has a direct connection with its aura.

Every action, significant or insignificant, intentional or unintentional, on the part of any person, creates relative impressions *(sanskaras),* which gets imprinted on the mind of the individual, just as sound is preserved on a gramaphone record and images of light and shade are caught on photographic plates. As thought is the first direct medium of expression of an impression, a deep connection is established between the thoughts and impressions of an individual.

An aura, therefore, is the mental reflection of the aggregate impressions of thoughts and actions, gathered by and stored in an individual mind. As long as the impressions are there, an aura is always there, as an envelope of subtle atmosphere, comprised of seven colors, which remain more or less prominent according to the nature of each individual's impressions.

No two men are alike in all respects, and yet all have common physical features. Similarly, the aggregate of individual impressions differ from one another, both quantitatively and qualitatively, yet every aura is comprised of seven colors, common to all. These seven colors of an individual's aura represent the seven principal categories, corresponding to the aggregate impressions of each individual.

Thus every individual aura is an image of a circle of seven colors. Each aura differs from the others in its proportion of each of the seven colors, according to the individual's predominant impressions. Likewise, each aura also differs in the color formation on the borders between every two predominant colors in it. For example, red would be the most prominent color in the aura of a man whose impressions are predominantly made up of lustful actions.

The halo begins to develop and an aura begins to disappear only after an individual starts advancing on the Path to God-Realization. When the aura begins to get more and more faint, the halo commences to shine more and more, getting brighter in proportion to the progress of the individual's consciousness on the Path. The halo becomes very bright only after an individual aura is on the point of disappearing. This happens in the case of a soul who wakes up fully conscious in the sixth plane of complete mental illumination.

In the Seventh Plane of Reality, the God-Realized One is, once and for all, entirely free from each and every impression, because the very storehouse of impressions itself, the individual mind, is then annihilated and there remains neither aura nor halo. The Reality of God alone remains supreme in the Self-Consciousness of Infinite Power, Infinite Knowledge and Infinite Bliss, with all illusion ceasing to remain as illusion.

When one who is God-Realized is able to return with his God-Consciousness simultaneously to all the planes of illusion as a Perfect Master, or Sadguru, his halo is then most bright—infinitely brighter than all the suns of the universe put together. It is out of the question for anyone, except those who have attained the consciousness of the Sixth Plane, to behold the Divine Effulgence of the Master's halo.

In all other cases the halo is an expression of individual advancement on the Path, and a sign of the dwindling of the individual's *sanskaras,* or impressions, in such cases, the halo is like a growing bright circle of the mental atmosphere of illumination, colorless throughout, and yet in every phase of its manifestation, far, far richer in spiritual splendor than any combination of colors can ever be.

Without going into further details, the table that follows will simplify the subject matter so far discussed.

Without necessarily being consciously advanced on the Path and only as a result of deep and sublime emotions, latent or expressed, the aspirant may have, from time to time, glimpses of the reflections of inner sights, reverberations of the echoes of inner sounds, redolences of the inner fragrances and distant shades of the inner ecstasies, all of which are but trivialities connected with the higher illusions of the Path. There are also many techniques and natural causes for the manifestation of such phenomena, which are beyond the faculties of an ordinary man. Volumes could be written, especially regarding the potentialities and repercussions of emotions both high and low.

For example, if, due to love for his Master, a man happens to see what appears to him as the halo of the Master, it is not actually the halo, but a part of his own aura as temporarily reflected by the effulgence of that halo—whether that of an Illuminated One or a Perfect Master.

All illusory phenomena, gross, subtle and mental, are not only dream-stuff, but everything termed in the table as "false-illusion" is made up of dream-into-dream stuff, which has no value at all, unless it helps man to awaken to Reality.

God is the only Reality, and all else is illusion. The whole of the gross universe is but part of the huge Cosmic Illusion, containing higher illusions of the Spiritual Planes of man's consciousness.

Real Birth and Real Death

There is one real birth and one real death. You are born once and you really die only once.

What is the real birth?

It is the birth of a "drop" in the Ocean of Reality. What is meant by the birth of a "drop" in the Ocean of Reality? It is the advent of individuality, born of indivisibility through a glimmer of the first most-finite consciousness, which transfixed cognizance of limitation into the Unlimited.

What is meant by the real death?

It is consciousness getting free of all limitations. Freedom from all limitations is real death: it is really the death of all limitations: it is liberation. In between the real birth and the real death, there is no such reality as the so-called births and deaths.

What really happens in the intermediate stage known as births and deaths is that the limitations of consciousness gradually wear off till it (consciousness) is free of all limitations. Ultimately, consciousness, totally free of all limitations, experiences the unlimited Reality eternally. Real dying is equal to real living. Therefore I stress: Die for God and you will live as God.

Fana

*Fana** is the state of unconscious consciousness. In *Fana* soul is unconscious of everything except Self being God.

Before the soul loses its human state and gains the divine state of *Nirvikalp,* it has to experience the vacuum state of *Nirvan.*

Nirvan is the infinite vacuum state when the soul is fully conscious of real Nothing.

Nirvan is immediately and inevitably followed by *Nirvikalp* or *Fana-fillah,* where the soul is fully conscious of real Everything. *Nirvan* and *Nirvikalp* are so irrevocably linked and tied together that each can be said to be the Divine Goal.

> False nothing = Illusory everything
> Real Nothing = Neither everything nor nothing
> Real Everything = God the Infinite

False nothing leads to false everything; and real Nothing leads to real Everything. False nothing is linked to false everything; and real Nothing is linked to real Everything. Eventually false nothing ends in false everything, and real Nothing ends in real Everything. In duality false nothing is false everything. In unity real Nothing and real Everything are one.

On the Living Dead

All beings on earth are in the Gross Sphere *(Anna-Bhumika,* or *Aalame-Nascot).* At the same time that does not mean that one cannot experience the other spheres of existence, nor that the earth by itself constitutes the whole of the gross sphere. Let us suppose, without taking the words "air" and "sky" and "sun" in their literal sense, that the Subtle Sphere *(Pran-Bhumika* or *Aalame-Malakoot)* exists in the "air"; that the Mental Sphere *(Mun-Bhumika* or *Aalame-Jabroot)* is situated in the "sky," and that the highest spiritual state *(Vidnyan-*

---

* The final annihilation of the mind

Bhumika or the *Arshe-Aala)* is in the "Sun," and that the "Sun" is all Power, all Knowledge and all Bliss, and is the Source of infinite beauty, sound, light, in fact, the Source of everything.

When it is said in Vedanta that the merging of the individual soul in the Oversoul results in the individual soul becoming the sun, the reference is to the transformation of the reflected or borrowed light into the very source of light itself and not to its literally becoming the sun that shines on earth. The sun visibly pervades the earth, air and sky and therefore analogically the sun is meant to be the very source of everything and the center of every circle. That is the reason why in Sufism a Perfect Master is recognized as the *Qutub,* i.e., the Center. In fact the position of every Perfect Master *(Sadguru* or *Qutub),* the Prophet or Avatar is in the "Sun," i.e., the *Vidnyan Bhumika,* the highest spiritual state.

The radiation of the Luster of the Eternal and Infinite Power which is the "Sun," first passes through the Mental Sphere and is made use of by those in the Mental Sphere. It then passes on through the Subtle Sphere where it is utilized by those in the Subtle Sphere. And finally the radiation filters through to the Gross Sphere where it shines as the third and dimmest reflection of the original Luster.

By the power, so to speak, borrowed from the Mental Sphere, those in the Subtle Sphere can easily read the thoughts of others in the same way as a man with gross eyes can almost effortlessly see anything and everything in the Gross Sphere.

With or without the gross body, those in the Subtle Sphere eat, drink and make use of their subtle bodies, possess clothes and even such things as neckties and other knick-knacks in the subtle form. They can and do utilize the power coming down to them from the Mental Sphere for the good and bad of others, as well as for their own, according to the individual nature and tendencies of each. Like the Saints *(Walis* or *Sants)* of the Mental Sphere possessing vast powers, those in the Subtle Sphere are also possessed of great powers, most particularly those on the Fourth Plane of spiritual splendour, who are among other things capable of raising the dead.

　　　　　　　　　　　　THE PATH OF LOVE

Hence arises the risk the Fourth Planers run of making grave misuse of these powers reflected to them through the Mental Sphere.

For example, if an ordinary man looks down from the heights of the Empire State Building in New York on to the streets below, he sees crowds of human beings looking as insignificant as a multitude of ants, mechanically moving hither and thither. In order to be able to attach due value to the ant-like masses of his fellow-beings, as they appear from these heights, he must necessarily come down amongst them. Similarly, those on the higher planes of the Subtle Sphere are apt to consider the Gross Sphere and all its activities as equally insignificant as that of the ants. Now, when a man happens to see a swarm of ants as feverishly busy as any crowd of human beings in a city Stock Exchange, he is not as a rule inclined to give them any serious consideration. But if by chance any of the ants happen to bite him, his reaction may take the turn of either forbearance or revenge. It might even tempt him to crush most of the ants if not all.

This illustration is only one aspect of the misuses of power. The Fourth Plane is the greatest hurdle of the spiritual Path, the crucial stage of the pilgrim's journey, where all is gained or lost. Great as are the powers at his command, greater are the temptations to use them for his own gratification, to exhibit these powers for the sake of display, for name, power, fame. For the ego, fearing complete defeat, rises to its highest, prodding and luring the pilgrim on to make selfish use of the powers lent to him. This lone fight with the hydra-headed ego is depicted in the paintings of the life of Buddha, and is known as the "dark night of the soul."

The pilgrim on the Fourth Plane is permitted, however, to make use of his powers for purely unselfish motives, with no thought whatever of self and only for the sake of others.

Although those in the Subtle Sphere derive their powers from the Mental Sphere, the misuse of these powers cannot be stopped by those in the Mental Sphere, because they originally radiated from the "Sun," the *Vidnyan Bhumika.* Therefore the Perfect Masters who as the Sun are themselves the very Source of Infinite

Power, are always there to snatch away, when necessary, the misused powers of those in the Subtle Sphere.

Like a murderer who, hanged unto death, is deprived not only of the power to do further mischief but also loses his life, so the Fourth Planer from whom a Perfect Master snatches away the powers, not only loses all powers but is automatically thrown back to the stage where the process of evolution of gross forms starts beyond that of the form of a stone!

That is why Kabir says, *"Chadhe to chakhe prem rus Aur giray to Chakna choor."* i.e., "He who climbs high enough, tastes the Nectar of Divine Love; but if he slips and falls, his utter ruin will ensue."

In contrast to those in the Subtle Sphere, those belonging to the Mental Sphere, whether on the Fifth or the Sixth Plane of superconsciousness, always use of their powers only for the good of others. They receive the direct radiation of the Divine Power, and those amongst them who are on the Sixth Plane—the Plane of "spiritual sight"—actually see God face to face. The paramount characteristic of these great souls of the Mental Sphere is that they are the real helpers behind the God-intoxicated *masts* who are so lost in God as to have next to no consciousness left of their gross existence. The bodies of these God-intoxicated lovers are sustained by the power of those in the Mental Sphere, the *Walis* and saints who are always face to face with God.

These *masts* who possess next to no physical consciousness and yet possess well-functioning bodies with which they eat, drink, walk and sleep, are the true spiritual heroes who are *dying and living at one and the same time.*

Although they care not a whit whether their bodies remain or fall, it is an established fact that their divine *"masti"* (God-intoxication) neutralizes the rigours of hunger, sleeplessness, heat, cold, disease and other onslaughts on the really care-free life led by these lovers of God. It is because the Infinite Power of the *Vidnyan Bhumika,* which vibrates throughout the universe, helps them.

There are only one hundred thousand *Sat-purushas* or *Marden-e-Khuda* (Men of God) in the whole of the universe. They are those on the Spiritual Path who have achieved control over their ego-life and who, with utter disregard to life, expose themselves to hardships in the name of, and for the sake of, God. It is not because these men and women of God find their lives to be any less precious than that of the average man or woman who, as a rule, is only too anxious to maintain a hold over the fast-slipping human life. Their indifference is due to the fact that to them their love for God is far greater than their own limited existence. It is not just a question of giving up a life "here" in order to gain a better life "there." To them nothing else remains worth while to be had or wished for, save their love for God.

In Vedanta and Sufism the certainty of God-Realization or Self-Experience is fully expounded. The *Vidnyan* or "I am God" state has to be actually experienced to be realized. After aeons, only one out of the hundred thousand wayfarers of the Path attain God-Realization. But in spite of the rarity of Perfection and the rigours involved in its attainment, every human being is perfectly capable of achieving it—in fact, is inevitably bound to do so, eventually. The knowledge of such a glorious certainty should cause man optimism rather than pessimism.

The God-conscious *Majzoobs* are conscious of nothing save the "I am God" state (*Aham Brahma Asmi* or *Anal Haq*). They are oblivious of their bodies, which continue to exist in all the three spheres, gross, subtle and mental. Being in the Eternal and Infinite *Vidnyan Bhumika,* their bodily existence is automatically and spontaneously sustained by their own Divinity. For some time after merging into the "Sun," they actually remain alive in the world; they continue to breathe, eat, drink, sleep, and do what an ordinary man can do.

They are truly the "Living Dead," for they are dead to the world, and yet to themselves are alive for all time. They are the Perfect Ones who have consumed death itself; and about whom Kabir says, *"Tan tyage, tan rahe; tan rakhe, tan jai. Yehi achamba hamne dekha, mada kal ko khai."* i.e. "Give up the body and it will remain; try to retain it and it will go."

The marvel of it is that the truly "dead" annihilate death itself.

Planes of Consciousness
in the Next Incarnation

Do persons on the spiritual planes of consciousness take birth having consciousness of the same plane? Yes, but the consciousness is very gradual, as when a person of gross-consciousness dies and is reborn with consciousness of the gross world. The child gradually becomes aware, as it grows older, of the same old gross world according to past experiences of the gross. A child born with consciousness of a certain plane is not all at once conscious of the plane. The plane unfolds very gradually as the child gradually grows. Later in life, this child, grown up as a man, gets established in the life of his respective plane-consciousness, as a man of the gross world gets established in his worldly life. Thus, a person of the gross world dies to reincarnate as of the gross world; so also a person of a particular plane of consciousness reincarnates as of that respective plane of consciousness and, then gradually gets established in the plane of consciousness of his previous life. He may or may not make further progress in the planes of higher consciousness. Progress will depend on the help of a spiritual guide of a higher plane, on the grace of a Perfect Master, or on his own efforts in the life of that particular plane of consciousness.

The Inexorable "Must"

Everything and everyone in the universe is constrained to move along a path which is prescribed by its past. There is an inexorable "must" that reigns over all things large or small. Whether one is male or female, rich or poor, strong or weak, beautiful or ugly, intelligent or dull—one cannot escape from being such because one *must* necessarily be so due to the impressions of the past.

The freedom which man seems to enjoy is itself subject to inner compulsions; and the environmental pressure, which limits the scope of reactions or molds the reacting self, is itself subject to the inexorable "must," which is operative in the past, present and future.

Man has his name, his sex, his personality, his color,

his nationality, his characteristics, his pain and pleasure and all that he may possess because he *must* have all these.

This overpowering compulsion is exercised by the force of innumerable impressions gathered in the past. These accumulated impressions cloud the consciousness of the "self" at every stage, in every incarnation of the future, which, in one's life, belongs to one's living present.

The rule of this inexorable "must" governs and re-shapes the so-called destiny of man in every incarnation as long as the "self" of man remains conscious of impressions. The principle of "must" which overrides human plans is based on divine law which both adjusts and gets adjusted by evolutionary impressions. It is only the divine will that can supersede the divine law.

The so many deaths during the one whole life, beginning from the evolution of consciousness to the end of the involution of consciousness, are like so many sleeps during one lifetime.

One who lives for himself is truly dead and one who dies for God is truly alive.

The Play of Ego

I

For one to declare that he is a saint and allow people to bow down to and revere him without real authority is to feed one's ego with intense happiness. Simultaneously, with the feeding of the ego comes a feeling of well-being.

One who is addicted to opium (eating or smoking) derives a similar feeling of well-being, though temporarily. After a time the opium-addict begins to feel the after-effects of opium in severe constipation, loss of appetite, headache, dullness and drowsiness. He then begins to realize that it would have been better had he not become addicted. But unfortunately, he cannot give up the habit. He has become a slave. He realizes this too late, and sinks into deeper addiction, being tempted to take greater and greater quantities of opium to keep pace with the gradual loss of the feeling of well-being.

Similarly, one who indulges in happiness by allowing people to bow down to him without authority, feels the prick of conscience later on. And, with this feeling he realizes that he has no authority, but has got so used to the habit of feeding his ego in this manner that he is unable to stop the practice. He continues indulging, and after a time does not pay heed to the pricks of conscience. He becomes numb to the voice within.

After years of addiction it so happens one day that the opium addict is found lying unconscious in a gutter full of filth. An extra overdose of opium proves tragic for the addict, who loses complete control over himself. The passer-by scoffs, ridicules, points at him as a confirmed opium addict.

In the same way, a person who poses as a saint, without really being one, starts to behave in an unworthy manner after years of indulgence in addiction to over-doses of homage. With him, contrary to the opium addict, his unworthy behavior is accounted as "perfection" by his followers! When he abuses others, his words are accepted as blessings! When he beats someone, his beating is accepted as the descent of his grace! When he indulges in love-making with the opposite sex, it is accepted as pure love! In short, whatever he does, all and everything is accepted in a spirit of reverence and love by the followers of the man who has posed as a saint. The more unruly his behavior the greater the admiration of the followers. And the greater the admiration the richer becomes the feeding of the ego of the person. Eventually, he falls from the high pedestal of admiration because, not being a genuine saint, the rich doses of admiration and reverence prove too much for the ego to digest! With the fall this "opiumized" saint is ridiculed. Those very persons, who called themselves his followers, scoff and call him a fraud.

Just as an opium addict has his personal friends who extol the effect of opium and bring into their fold innocent people, so, too, a person who poses as a saint has a ring of followers who extol him and his "miracles" to attract others to their fold. Such miracles may be just coincidences or even genuine experiences of simple and devout followers, who get desired results through their own faith in and love even for such "opiumized" saints.

II.

One who has no authority and yet permits people to bow down to him plays a losing game, while those who bow down gain. The unburdening of *sanskaras* of those who bow down at his feet is the cause of his loss, for he takes on *sanskaras* that can only be wiped off by many more births.

The point to be considered is this: if thousands can benefit at the cost of a false saint should this person be allowed to continue?

If such a person is already in contact with a Perfect Master and loves him, the Master immediately puts a check and corrects the shortcomings and warns his lovers about such unauthorized behavior.

If, however, such a person is not already in contact with a Perfect Master, the Master never interferes, because eventually this person also derives some benefit. The Master knows that this is the play of ego. The cause of any eventual benefit to such a person is that at the cost of his own condemnation he proved to be a dust-bin for thousands to help their *sanskaras* therein.

There is no doubt that in his subsequent birth his behavior makes the person suffer much more due to this burden of acquired *sanskaras*. But with the intensity of his suffering, the redeeming factor is the speed with which these acquired *sanskaras* get wiped off. They are wiped off in proportion to the intensity of suffering. Along with the wiping off of the acquired *sanskaras,* his own *sanskaras* also get wiped off speedily.

III.

Just as an unauthorized person, posing as a saint, proves a source of benefit to thousands, so also he proves of harm to many. All this is a play in illusion!

As an opium-addict feels happy to give a tiny bit of opium to another, and that other, when he gets the taste of it, hands over another small dose to his own friend, creating a circle of opium-eaters, the two or three persons, close to the 'opiumized' saint of our discourse, start spreading news that such and such a woman was blessed with a child, and that another got her wish fulfilled, and that the 'saint' performed many such miracles. A clique of followers around the 'opiumized' saint is created.

But this happy picture does not last long, for after some years it so happens that at least one finds out one day that his master is a fraud and is not God-realized. The impact of such a great set-back in his confirmed belief is so forceful that all his *sanskaras,* which he had inadvertently transferred on to the saint in his belief and devotion, all of a sudden recoil on him spontaneously and overburden him afresh. Thus the person who had placed faith in the "opiumized" saint suffers a great deal.

Let us view the picture from another angle: suppose I am the 'opiumized' saint and you love me and revere me as the Perfect Master. Your love becomes so deep and your faith so great that you actually make progress on the spiritual path, and really begin to have experiences of the path. In this instance, you are surely benefitted at the hands of 'opiumized' saint. Whereas in the previous case, 'opiumized' saint has done a great harm. Through such 'saints' harm and benefit recoil and accrue.

But all this is a play in illusion. It is all my play. None can fathom me as I really am. I am in everyone and I do everything; simultaneously, I also do nothing.

Be brave: Be happy: I and you are all One: And the Infinite that eternally belongs to me will one day belong to every individual.

On Split Ego or Split "I"

I.

Introducing the discourse on split "I" Baba said:

You must have heard about split personality. Stories have been developed on this theme. Most of you must have heard of Dr. Jekyll and Mr. Hyde—a combination of good and evil characters in one. It is an example of split personality.

Such a thing, to some extent, is common in all. One day a person feels happy and is in a buoyant mood; the same person, the next day or the next hour, may feel dejected and depressed. One day he does good actions; the next he is engaged in actions which are undesirable.

Just as there is split personality, so there is also split ego. All do not have a split personality, but all do have a split ego—"I." The real "I" of all is One. There is also false "I" in every individual, which gives rise to his separative existence. The infinite real "I," which is One and in all, is apparently split into innumerable, finite false "I's," giving rise to separative individualized existence.

In short, it is the One real "I" that plays the part of innumerable finite false "I's" in multifarious ways and in varying degrees.

The main support of false "I" is ignorance. False "I" utilizes three channels or means for its expressions—the gross body (the physical body), the subtle body (the energy), and the mental body (the mind).

In other words, with the support of ignorance the real "I" takes itself as false "I" and tries to derive fun out of the situation. In doing this, the false "I" continuously gets set-backs and endures great suffering. Eventually, the real "I" gets fed up and stops playing the part of false "I."

As soon as the real "I" stops playing the part of the false "I," it becomes conscious of its (real) pristine state. This consciousness is eternal. And it also realizes that, being eternally happy, its experience of being fed up was sheer nonsensical ignorance.

The real "I" when playing the part of false "I," whatever it does, sees, feels, thinks, understands, says, is false, because the false "I" is virtually false itself.

II.

The aim of all yogas is one. The aim is that the false ego or the falsity of the split ego should disappear and the real ego be manifested in its reality.

In other words, the real "I" which plays the part of the false "I" should completely forget to play the part and assert itself as it really is.

It becomes impossible for the real "I" to forget that it is playing the part of false "I." But the real "I" tries to forget the part it plays of the false "I" through action (*karma yoga*).

For example, take Eruch. His is the real "I" within, but as Eruch, he is the false "I." Now the real "I" within Eruch tries to forget that it is playing only the part of the false "I," as Eruch. While trying to do so, the false "I" as Eruch, tries its best to serve so many other false "I's." But the fun is that one false "I" in its struggle to forget, efface itself, remembers so many other false "I's," while bent upon serving them!

The One Real "I," which is eternally free, gets apparently bound by this process, and, it is eternally trying to forget and trying to remember at one and the same time.

In another type of yoga (*bhakti yoga*) the real "I," while acting the part of the false "I," tries to worship the real. The false "I" cannot be anything but false, and it cannot have any conception of the real "I." The real "I," acting as false "I," forms a false conception of the real "I."

Then what does the false "I" say? It says, "O Real I! I worship Thee in all!"

And the tragedy is that when the false "I" prays to and worships the real "I," it sees and comes across only the innumerable false "I's." In fact it worships other false "I's," rather than the One and Real "I."

However, the path of Love (*prem yoga*) is unique, because on it the Real "I" plays the part of the false "I," while it itself covertly remains in the background as the Beloved. And, while continuing to play this part, it burns or consumes its false ego, to remain ultimately itself as the Beloved.

In Eruch, for example, the real "I" acts as the false "I" and loves the real "I" within. On one hand there is the real "I" and on the other, there is the false "I" as Eruch. But these are not two separate "I's." The false "I" as Eruch, tries to bestow love on the real "I." And that is why with gradual increase in love and with greater intensity of longing, the false "I" by degrees gets more and more consumed, effaced, by love. All the while, the real "I," as the Beloved, remains in the background as it really is. Eventually, when the false "I" is totally consumed, there remains neither the false "I" nor love. The Beloved, as the real "I," reigns supreme as One Infinite Indivisible Self.

In the subtle planes, the inner experiences of the real "I" may be said to be Divine Hallucination. In the mental planes, the inner experiences of the real "I" may be said to be Spiritual Nightmare. Inner experiences end in Divine Awakening.

THREE

The Art of Discipleship

It is said the Master appears when one is ready. But how can one be ready for Perfection, and all its ways? Therefore Perfection, in the guise of the Master, must come down to the level of our imperfection, and help us to be the true disciple. That is why, at times, the Master often plays the role of the disciple. He shows, not tells, us how to behave—especially in relation to him. The following are a few of the invaluable hints to the seeker, from the One who is sought.

Twelve Ways of Realizing Me

The MASTER points out twelve ways in which the spiritual Seeker may realize his own Divine Self, which is One within all and which is completely manifested in the Perfect Master.

1. LONGING . . .
If you experience that same longing and thirst for Union with Me as one who has been lying for days in the hot sun of the Sahara experiences the longing for water, then you will realize Me.

2. PEACE OF MIND . . .
If you have the peace of a frozen lake, then too, you will realize Me.

3. HUMILITY . . .
If you have the humility of the earth which can be molded into any shape, then you will know Me.

4. DESPERATION . . .
If you experience the desperation that causes a man to commit suicide and you feel that you cannot live without seeing Me, then you will see Me.

5. FAITH . . .
If you have the complete faith that Kalyan had for his Master, in believing it was night, although it was day, because his Master said so, then you will know Me.

6. FIDELITY . . .
If you have the fidelity that the breath has in giving you company, even without your constantly feeling it, till the end of your life, that both in happiness and in suffering gives you company and never turns against you, then you will know Me.

7. CONTROL THROUGH LOVE . . .
When your love for Me drives away your lust for the things of the senses, then you realize Me.

8. SELFLESS SERVICE . . .

If you have the quality of selfless service unaffected by results, similar to that of the sun which serves the world by shining on all creation, on the grass in the field, on the birds in the air, on the beasts in the forest, on all mankind with its sinner and its saint, its rich and its poor, unconscious of their attitude towards it, then you will win Me.

9. RENUNCIATION . . .

If you renounce for Me everything physical, mental and spiritual, then you have Me.

10. OBEDIENCE . . .

If your obedience is spontaneous, complete and natural as the light is to the eye or smell is to the nose, then you come to Me.

11. SURRENDER . . .

If your surrender to Me is as wholehearted as that of one, who, suffering from insomnia, surrenders to sudden sleep without fear of being lost, then you have Me.

12. LOVE . . .

If you have that love for Me that St. Francis had for Jesus, then not only will you realize Me, but you will please Me.

The High Roads to God

In an important sense, all walks of life and all Paths ultimately lead but to one goal, *viz.,* God. All rivers enter into the Ocean, in spite of the diverse directions in which they flow, and in spite of the many meanderings which characterize their paths. However, there are certain *High Roads, which take the pilgrim directly to his Divine Destination.* They are important, because they avoid prolonged wanderings in the wilderness of complicated by-ways, in which the pilgrim is often unnecessarily caught up.

The rituals and ceremonies of organized religions can lead the seeker only to the *threshold of the true Inner Journey, which proceeds along certain High Roads.* These remain distinct from each other, for a very considerable distance, though towards the end they all get merged in each other. In the earlier phases, they remain distinct, owing to the diversity of *sanskaric* contexts of individuals and the differences of their temperaments. In any case, it should be clear from the very beginning that though the Roads may be many, the Goal is and always will be only one, *viz.,* attainment of union with God.

The quickest of these High Roads lies through the God-man, who is consciously one with the Truth. In the God-man, God reveals himself in all His Glory, with His Infinite Power, Unfathomable Knowledge, Inexpressible Bliss and Eternal Existence. The Path through the God-man is available only to those fortunate ones who approach him in *complete surrenderance and unwavering faith.* Complete surrenderance to the God-man, is, however, possible only to very advanced aspirants. But when this is not possible, the other High Roads, which can eventually win the Grace of God, are:

1) Love for God and intense longing to see Him and to be united with Him

2) Being in constant company with the saints and lovers of God and rendering them wholehearted service

3) Avoiding lust, greed, anger, hatred and the temptations for power, fame and fault-finding

4) Leaving everyone and everything in complete external renunciation, and in solitude, devoting oneself to fasting, prayer and meditation

5) Carrying on all worldly duties with equal acceptance of success or failure, with a pure heart and clean mind and remaining unattached in the midst of intense activity

6) Selfless service of humanity, without any thought of gain or reward

Dissertation on Love

What is Love? To give and never to ask. What leads to this Love? Grace. What leads to this Grace? Grace is not cheaply bought. It is gained by being always ready to serve and reluctant to be served. There are many points which lead to this Grace:

> *Wishing well for others at the cost of one's self.*
> *Never backbiting.*
> *Tolerance supreme.*
> *Trying not to worry. Trying not to worry is almost impossible—so try!*
> *Thinking more of the good points in others and less of their bad points.*

What leads to this Grace? Doing all the above. If you do one of these things perfectly, the rest must follow. Then Grace descends. Have Love—and when you have Love, the union with the Beloved is certain.

When Christ said, "Love your neighbor," he did not mean fall in love with your neighbor.

When you love, you give; when you fall in love, you want. Love me in any way you like, but love me. It is all the same. Love me. I am pure, the Source of purity, so I consume all weaknesses in my fire of Love. Give your sins, weaknesses, virtues, all to me—but give. I would not mind even one falling in love with me—I can purify; but when you fall in love with anybody else, you cannot call it love. Love is pure as God. It gives and never asks; that needs Grace.

Yogis in the Himalayas, with their long eyelashes and long beards, meditating, sitting in *Samadhi,* they too, have not this Love . . . it is so precious. The mother dies for her child—supreme sacrifice, yet it is not Love. Heroes die for their country, but that is not Love.

Love! You know when you have Love. You cannot understand theoretically, you have to experience it.

Mainu loved Leila. This was pure Love, not physical, not intellectual, but spiritual Love. He saw Leila in everything and everywhere. He never thought of eating, drinking, sleeping, without thinking of her, and all the time he wanted her happiness. He would have gladly seen her married to another if he knew that would make her happy, and die for her husband if he thought she would be happy in that. At last it led him to me—no thought of self, but of the beloved, every second and continually.

You would not be able to do that if you tried. It needs Grace.

Trying leads to Grace.
What is God?
Love.
Infinite Love is God.

Sahavas

Sahavas is the intimacy of give and take of love.

I am the only Beloved and you all are my lovers; or I am the only Lover and you all are my beloveds.

I want you all to remain happy in my Sahavas. This will be the last Sahavas. I am the Ocean of Love. Draw as much of this love as possible. Make the most of this opportunity. It rests with you to draw as much love as possible out of the Ocean. It does not rest with Me to explain to you how you should love me. Does a husband or a wife explain to one another how to love? One thing is certain; I want to give you my love. It depends on each of you to receive it. The easy way to receive it is to forget your home, family and all worldly affairs, when you are here, and be receptive to my love. This is the first thing to follow if you want to receive the maximum of my love. The second thing to follow is to have a good night's rest, sleep well each night and feel fresh when you come here for my Sahavas each day. I am God: if you remain drowsy in my presence, you will miss me and your drowsiness will oblige you to remain absent from my presence, in spite of your daily attendance.

Sahavas means intimate companionship. To establish this companionship you should be free with me. Sahavas is the intimacy of give and take of love between the lovers and the Beloved. There is no need to explain this give and take of love. To create an atmosphere of explanations and discourses is to mar the dignity of love which is established only in the closest of intimacy.

How do I participate in the Sahavas? I bow down to myself. I embrace myself. It is I who smile, who weep: it is Baba who sits here on the dais seat and it is Baba who squats on the ground in the tent. Baba meets 'Baba': Baba consoles 'Baba,' pets 'Baba,' chides 'Baba.' It is all Baba, Baba, Baba. Such is my experience of participation in the Sahavas.

Drink deep at the fountain of love, but do not lose consciousness! If you can but taste even a drop of this love—what a wonderful experience it will be! Have you any idea what this Sahavas is? He who approaches me with a heart full of love, has my Sahavas. After I drop this body and my passing away from your midst, many things will be said about this Sahavas. Take fullest advantage of this opportunity in the living presence of the Avatar. Forget everything else but my Sahavas and concentrate all your attention on me. I am the Ancient One.

Seven Sahavas Sayings

Desire for nothing except desirelessness.
> Hope for nothing except to rise above all hopes.
> Want nothing and you will have everything.

Seek not to possess anything but to surrender everything.
> Serve others with the understanding that in them you are serving me.
> Be resigned completely to my will and my will will be yours.
> Let nothing shake your faith in me and all your bindings will be shaken off.

Real happiness lies in making others happy.
> The real desire is that which leads you to become perfect in order to make others perfect.
> The real aim is that which aims to make others become God by first attaining Godhood yourself.

Be angry with none but your weakness.
> Hate none but your lustful self.
> Be greedy to own more and more wealth of tolerance and justice.
> Let your temptation be to tempt me with your love in order to receive my grace.
> Wage war against your desires and Godhood will be your victory.

Love others as you would love yourself and all that is yours.

Fortunate are they whose love is tested by misfortunes.
Love demands that the lover sacrifice for the Beloved.

Real living is dying for God.
Live less for yourself and more for others.
One must die to one's own self to be able to live in all other selves.
One who dies for God lives forever.

This period of Sahavas is the period of my suffering and helplessness.
My glorification will follow my humiliation.

On Obedience

Giving an introduction to His discourse on different types of obedience, Baba said: In one of his couplets Hafiz says, "How can you step on the Path of Truth unless you step out of the boundary of your own nature?" Baba continued: The Path of God-realization has untold and intolerable hardships and suffering. Even yogis, saints and *Satpurushas* are unable to fathom My reality. Hafiz speaks of stepping out of the boundary of one's own nature before one dares to step on to the path of reality. But what is one's own nature?

I am not going to repeat the theme of evolution of forms and consciousness, which has been explained at length in *God Speaks*. Best to begin this discourse with the birth of a child: the child takes birth according to his past *karma (sanskaras* or *impressions).* He will act, think, feel according to his *sanskaras* gathered in past lives; there is no way out of it for the child. This is what I call the law of "must." This law sticks to the child from birth to death. It has formulated the nature of the child, and has become the child's very nature. The child cannot get out of it. In addition to this inexorable law of must, the environmental circumstances of the child are such that he cannot but act and feel according to the impressions of the experiences of past lives. When the baby is born, it must cry; mother must feed the baby; its very sex is determined by the law of must. If the baby is a male child, it is so because it must be born a male child; if it is a female child, it is so because it must be born a female. And when the child grows into a man or woman, it becomes what it does become because it must be so.

Do not confuse this nature with Nature—the entire panorama of the earth and its seasons! Your nature is the nature created by you and nurtured by you. It is one's own nature that is responsible for the body one takes on—the shape, the complexion, the health, sickness, appetite, temperament, etc. In short, anything and everything connected with one's own self—physical, subtle and mental.

Now to return to the difficulties on the Path. I say that it is impossible even for one on the Path to fathom my real state: why is it impossible? Hafiz said that unless one steps out of the limitations of one's own nature (routine of life), one cannot step on to the Path of reality. Here realization of reality is obviously not meant. What Hafiz means is that it is impossible to realize your real self as long as you are bound within the limitations of your own nature. This means that you should go against your very nature, against the very nature of your physical, subtle and mental bodies!

Thus, if you are hungry, you should not eat; if you are not hungry, you should eat! When you feel like sleeping, you should not sleep; when you do not feel like sleeping, you should sleep! This is what Hafiz means by going against one's own nature—stepping out of the boundary of your nature. Again, if you wish to see anything, you should not; and if you do not wish to see, you should see. When you exert yourself, you pant; but you should not pant, you should feel normal. Your breathing should be a normal breathing, just when you are out of breath. You are sitting, silently listening to this discourse and your breathing is normal; it must not be so —according to the couplet of Hafiz. From all this you will understand how impossible it is to go against your own nature and realize me as I really am.

But, here, Hafiz himself comes to your rescue and says that there is a solution: this solution too is most difficult, but at least it is less impossible. In another of his couplets Hafiz says, "O You, if you ever get possessed by madness to realize God, then become the dust at the feet of a Perfect Master—*Qutub* or *Sadguru*." Hafiz uses the word "madness' to depict, once again, that it is a sheer impossibility to realize this state of reality. The question now arises as to how should one become dust at the feet of a Perfect Master.

Dust has not thought of its own, whether it is trampled upon, or applied to the forehead of a man, or remains suspended in air or water. It is all one and the same to it. I tell you that there is no truer and better example of complete obedience than becoming like dust.

Baba remarked: Those who cannot follow this discourse should not worry: just concentrate on me. Words have no real value. It is good if you can understand: if you do not, why worry?

Summing up this discourse, Baba repeated what a Sufi poet had said: "After years and years of longing for Union with God, only one, out of a million *Mardan-e-Khuda* (Men of God), realized God."

In the end, Baba gave assurance by saying: Be brave. Be happy. I and you all are One. And the Infinite that eternally belongs to me will one day belong to every individual. (Baba pointed out that it was incorrect to say: "You all and I are One"; the truth is "I and you all are One.")

Surrender

He who genuinely surrenders to a Perfect Master surrenders completely without asking for permission to do so. He does not even expect acceptance of his surrender from the Master. Complete surrender in itself embodies the acceptance of one who has surrendered completely as he ought to have done.

The Lover and the Beloved

Beloved God is in all.

What is then the duty of the lover?

It is to make the Beloved happy without sparing himself. Without giving a second thought to his own happiness the lover should seek the pleasure of the Beloved. The only thought a lover of God should have is to make the Beloved happy.

Thus if you stop thinking of your own happiness and give happiness to others, you will then indeed play the part of the lover of God, because Beloved God is in all.

But, while giving happiness to others, if you have an iota of thought of self, it is then not love but affection. This tends to seek happiness for the self while making others happy.

As an example: (1) A husband's affection for his wife. The husband wants to give happiness to his wife; but while doing so he thinks of his own happiness, too. (2) A mother's affection for her child. From this affection the mother derives happiness purely out of giving and seeking happiness for her child.

Love and Devotion

Love burns the lover.
> Devotion burns the Beloved.

Love seeks happiness for the Beloved.
> Devotion seeks for blessing from the Beloved.

Love seeks to shoulder the burden of the Beloved.
> Love gives. Devotion asks.

Love is silent and sublime, devoid of outward expressions.
> Devotion expresses itself outwardly.

Love does not require the presence of the Beloved in order to love.
> Devotion demands the presence of the Beloved to express affection for the Beloved.

Love is the Remedy

Do not give undue importance to explanations and discourses. Words fail to give any meaning to Reality; because when one supposes that one has understood, one has not understood: one is far from understanding anything so far as Reality is concerned. Reality is beyond human understanding *(Samaj)* for it is beyond intellect. Understanding cannot help because God is beyond understanding. The moment you try to understand God you "misunderstand" Him; you miss Him when you try to understand Him. Intellect must go before knowledge dawns.

All this is a show, a fun *(Tamasha),* a play. Mind must go, because the fun lies in the mind. And the fun is that mind must annihilate itself. Only *Man-O-Nash* (annihilation of mind) takes one to Reality. If I tell you to jump over another person you can do it; but you cannot jump over yourself: at the most you would turn a somersault: but there is a way to annihilate the mind. The way is love. Just consider ordinary human love: when a man or a woman is deeply in love with his or her partner, nothing comes between them. They get totally lost in love for one another. There is neither admiration nor fault-finding. There is total absence even of exchange of thought: love prevails without thoughts. Mind becomes defunct for the time being: for in such intense human love mind does not come into play. The mind apparently gets annihilated for the fraction of a second when love and loving are at their zenith. This brings about a state similar to trance. If ordinary human love can go so far, what should be said of the height of love divine?

I am the Ancient One, the One residing in every heart. Therefore, love others, make others happy, serve others, even at discomfort to yourself; this is to love me. I suffer for the whole universe. I must suffer infinitely: unless I suffered how could I ask my lovers to suffer for others? I am One with all on every level: I am One with all on every plane of consciousness: and I am beyond all planes of consciousness.

My Wish

Baba said: The lover has to keep the wish of the Beloved. My wish for my lovers is as follows:

1. Do not shirk your responsibilities.
2. Attend faithfully to your worldly duties, but keep always at the back of your mind that all this is Baba's.
3. When you feel happy, think: "Baba wants me to be happy." When you suffer, think: "Baba wants me to suffer."
4. Be resigned to every situation and think honestly and sincerely: "Baba has placed me in this situation."
5. With the understanding that Baba is in everyone, try to help and serve others.

6. I say with my Divine Authority to each and all that whosoever take my name at the time of breathing his last comes to me: so do not forget to remember me in your last moments. Unless you start remembering me from now on, it will be difficult to remember me when your end approaches. You should start practicing from now on. Even if you take my name only once every day, you will not forget to remember me in your dying moments.

How to Love God

To love God in the most practical way is to love our fellow beings. If we feel for others in the same way as we feel for our own dear ones, we love God.

If, instead of seeing faults in others, we look within ourselves, we are loving God.

If, instead of robbing others to help ourselves, we rob ourselves to help others, we are loving God.

If we suffer in the sufferings of others and feel happy in the happiness of others, we are loving God.

If, instead of worrying over our own misfortunes, we think ourselves more fortunate than many many others, we are loving God.

If we endure our lot with patience and contentment, accepting it as His Will, we are loving God.

If we understand and feel that the greatest act of devotion and worship to God is not to hurt or harm any of His beings, we are loving God.

To love God as He ought to be loved, we must live for God and die for God, knowing that the goal of life is to Love God, and find Him as our own self.

On Baba's Work

Baba is the Avatar of the Age and the greatest work anyone can do is to love Baba as Baba ought to be loved. He alone who can love Baba does Baba's work. What is Baba's work? It is to tell people who Baba is and that Baba says one should love all, slander none, have a pure heart and not make others suffer for one's own comfort and pleasure. If Baba's workers themselves lack these qualities, how can they tell others of what Baba says, and work as Baba's workers? On the contrary, such workers have no share in doing Baba's work. They are a burden in Baba's work.

There are two types of workers. There is one who tells people who Baba is and what Baba says, and himself lives and acts as I want my worker to be in life. There is another, who also loves me, in his own way, and lacks the qualities desired by me. When such a one, instead of doing my work haphazardly, confesses his incapacity to others, and tells them what I want them to do, there is no binding created for the workers and no burden felt by me on behalf of such a worker. The worker should be bold and candid enough to admit and try to overcome his weaknesses before he attempts to preach what Baba says.

In doing Baba's work there is one great difficulty. The workers have love for Baba, no doubt, but at the same time they have their characteristic weaknesses. The great difficulty resides in the expression of one's ego—the feeling of self-importance by which one is possessed, despite one's best efforts to lose it. The heart is for weakening the ego, but the mind is for strengthening it. The mind gains a sense of greatness in doing Baba's work. There is no escaping this. What is to be done then? Try to be humble? But even when the leader of a group charged with the responsibility of spreading Baba's message of love tries to be humble, his co-workers may take it as a mere posing on the part of their leader and look down upon him; though for his quality of leadership other people respect the leader.

Another weak spot in doing Baba's work is that the workers themselves fail to cooperate. With differences of opinion they find fault with one another. The result is that the work itself suffers. All this is because the workers differ among themselves while they dare to carry to the people Baba's message of Love and Truth and Purity of heart!

But there is a remedy for this type of disunity. If the workers tried to act upon it sincerely, it would be easy to wipe away the weak spot. Real workers are those who, in addition to giving help to their leaders, disregard the faults of their leaders and co-workers. In such cases, the workers themselves become leaders, and yet remain sincere workers too. If my workers follow this advice, and cooperate with their leaders and co-workers, understanding that it is I who have entrusted the responsibility to the group-heads, then your Baba's work would be done.

How to Escape Illusion

My message today, to those who love me, and believe in my life, is that in order to escape this cosmic Illusion, and to realize and attain the supreme Reality, we must abide by the following:

First and foremost, our complete surrender to the God-man, in whom God reveals Himself in His full glory, His infinite power, His unfathomable knowledge, His inexpressible bliss, and His eternal existence.

Should this complete surrender not be possible, then one or some of the following, if faithfully carried out, can win the grace of God:

(1) Wholehearted love for God. Thirst for seeing Him, longing to know Him and burning desire for union with Him, constitutes this all-consuming love for which the lover forsakes everything, including himself.

(2) Keeping constant company with saints and lovers of God, and rendering them wholehearted service.

(3) Guarding the mind against temptations of lust, greed, anger, hatred, power, fame and fault-finding.

(4) Absolute and complete external renunciation whereby one leaves everyone and everything, and in solitude devotes oneself to prayer, fasting and meditation.

(5) Living in the world and yet practicing complete internal renunciation. This means attending to all worldly duties without attachment, knowing all to be an illusion and only God to be real, carrying out one's worldly affairs with a pure heart and clean mind, and living the life of a recluse in the midst of intense activity.

(6) Selfless service. One who practices this, thinks not of himself but of the happiness of others, serves others with no thought of gain or reward, never allows

the mind to be upset or disappointed; and facing all odds and difficulties cheerfully, sacrifices his welfare for the good of others. This is the life of the selfless worker.

The Master's Prayer

O Parvardigar, the preserver and protector of all,
You are without beginning, and without end;
Non-dual, beyond comparison; and none can measure You.
You are without color, without expression, without form, and without attributes.
You are unlimited and unfathomable, beyond imagination and conception; eternal and imperishable.
You are indivisible; and none can see You, but with eyes divine.
You always were, You always are, and You always will be;
You are everywhere, You are in everything; and You are also beyond everywhere and beyond everything.
You are in the firmament and in the depths, You are manifest and unmanifest; on all planes, and beyond all planes.
You are in the three worlds, and also beyond the three worlds;
You are imperceptible and independent.
You are the Creator, the Lord of Lords, the knower of all minds and hearts; You are ominipotent and omnipresent.
You are Knowledge Infinite, Power Infinite, and Bliss Infinite.
You are the Ocean of Knowledge, all-knowing, infinitely knowing; the knower of the past, the present and the future, and You are Knowledge itself.
You are all-merciful and eternally benevolent;
You are the Soul of souls, the One with infinite attributes;
You are the trinity of Truth, Knowledge, and Bliss;
You are the Source of Truth, the Ocean of Love;
You are the Ancient One, the Highest of the High; You are Prabhu and Parameshwar; You are the Beyond-God, and the Beyond-Beyond-God also; You are

Parabrahma; Allah; Elahi; Yezdan; Ahuramazda; and God the Beloved.

You are named Ezad: *i.e.,* the only One worthy of worship.

The Prayer of Repentance

We repent, O God most merciful; for all our sins; for every thought that was false or unjust or unclean; for every word spoken that ought not to have been spoken; for every deed done that ought not to have been done.

We repent for every deed and word and thought inspired by selfishness, and for every deed and word and thought inspired by hatred.

We repent most specially for every lustful thought and every lustful action; for every lie; for all hypocrisy; for every promise given but not fulfilled, and for all slander and backbiting.

Most specially also, we repent for every action that has brought ruin to others; for every word and deed that has given others pain; and for every wish that pain should befall others.

In your unbounded mercy we ask You to forgive us, O God! for all these sins committed by us, and to forgive us for our constant failures to think and speak and act according to Your will.

On Worry

I will begin the talk by telling you *not to worry!* Whatever suffering may befall you, you should put up with it with full faith in and love for Baba. At the most what could happen? You might die. And it is so very obvious that you have to die one day; you have to drop this body sooner or later. Why not then think that your body is not there already and so act detached? One more thing you must remember: that is, be honest. I am in everyone and in everything. God is in everyone and in everything. And, because God is in everyone and everything, He knows everything. So be resigned completely to His will.

* * *

Once you were a child; now your have grown up. During the period from childhood up to now you have gone through moments of great joys and sorrows. Where has all that gone? The fact is neither joy nor sorrow was there; it is due to *maya* that you think of and experience things, which have no foundation. Within 20 or 30 years you will also forget the thoughts and events of today. So the best thing for you to do is just to love me. Love me honestly, work for me, I alone endure; all else is but a passing show! There should not be any trace of show in the work you do for me. You should have no expectations of reward for any work you do. In fact, I am much pleased and happy with your love and work. Don't worry.

* * *

Do not worry. Be happy in my Love and continue to hold fast to my *daaman** to the very end. Rest assured that all will be divinely well. God does not abandon those who trust Him. Those who love me and obey me as I should be loved and obeyed, will one day be similarly loved and obeyed. Those who have today willingly chosen to become my slaves, will become true masters tomorrow.

* * *

D_____, are you worried? Didn't you hear what Hafiz said—not to grieve? Who else is worried? *No one answered.* If no one is worrying, *Baba gestured,* I have to worry. But my worry is great fun for me! It's a very old habit of mine to worry for the whole creation, to worry continuously for the release of souls from the bondage of life and death. It's great fun. Some come to me to heal their diseases, to bless them with better prospects in life, or for a job or for children, or because they have too many children! And I have to worry about all those things, in addition to my universal worries. You see me

* *hem of the Master's garment*

sitting here with you, but I am simultaneously on all the planes of consciousness, on all those stations on the chart* that is here before you. There are souls in the Subtle World who want me—and I am there with them; and there are those in the Mental World who want me, and I am there with them. You are in the Gross World, so you find me with you in the Gross World; those in the Subtle World find me in the Subtle World, those in the Mental World find me in the Mental World. And one rare one who finds me as I really am is blessed . . . But remember not to worry! Take the advice of Hafiz and do not worry!

*   *   *

Don't worry. Worry accumulates and grows in strength, becomes a habit long after the original cause has ceased to be. When you were young, this and that happened, you cried, you felt sad, and worry began, and after 50 years you still worry, although the time when worry began in you has gone. If another 50 years passes you could at the end of that time be still worrying about something which was happening now. It is crazy.

You worry now about some condition, yet you have experienced all conditions. You have been blind, sick, poor, old, young, beautiful, ugly. You worry about your children—you have had numberless children, and they have had numberless parents and children. You worry about your job—you have been in every sort of occupation. You worry about your wife—you have had so many wives. You have been everything and experienced all conditions, and yet you worry about the slightest thing that happens to you.

*   *   *

Everything emanates from me but is not real. If you were dreaming and I appeared in your dream and told you you were dreaming, it is not real, you would say,

* a chart depicting the Four Journeys. vid *The Everything and the Nothing*

"Baba, I am enjoying these things, I know they are real."
It is hard to understand. In your awake dream, I tell you
now, nothing is real, so don't worry. How to stop? Think
of me. Love me. Christ said with Divine Authority,
"Your sins are forgiven"; and I say with Divine Authority, "Love me, and your worries will vanish."

Reality is impossible to describe—it is difficult to
attain. One in a million becomes a lover of God and of a
million lovers one gets Realization. It sounds impossible.
Baba says, you have an opportunity because I am here
with you and I say, "Love me."

* * *

Duality signifies separateness. Separateness implies
fear. Fear causes worry.

The way of Oneness is the way to happiness. The
way of manyness leads to worries. I am the only One
without a second; so I am eternally happy. You are
separate from your Self; so you always worry. To you,
what you see is absolutely real; to me it is absolutely false.
I alone am real and my *marjee* (will) governs the cosmic
Illusion.

It is the truth when I say that the waves do not roll or
the leaves do not move without my will. The moment the
intensity of your faith in my will reaches the apex, you bid
adieu to worry for good. Then, all that you suffered and
enjoyed in the past, together with all that you may experience in the future, will be to you the most loving and
spontaneous expression of my will; and, as the lover
places the will of the Beloved above all else, there is
nothing which can cause worry.

Live more and more in the present which is ever
beautiful and which really stretches far beyond the limits
of the past and the future. If at all you want to worry, let
your only worry be: how to remember me constantly.
This is worth worrying about, because it is the antidote
for worry.

Think of me more and more, and all your worries
will dwindle into nothing, for they are really nothing, and
my will works out to awaken this in you and in all.

Baba's Sermon

Being just now in the "Old Life" for these few hours,* I will tell you what I feel to be the established divine facts:

Essentially we are all one. The feeling of our being otherwise is due to ignorance. Soul desires consciousness to know itself, but in its progress towards this Goal which it cannot realize independently of creation, it must undergo the experience which it gathers as the individualized ego and which is all imagination. Thus it is faced at the outset with ignorance instead of Knowledge.

Dual forms and illusionary creations are the outcome of ignorance: birth and death, happiness and misery, virtue and sin, good and bad—all are equally the manifestation of this same ignorance. You were never born and will never die; you never suffered and will never suffer; you ever were and ever will be, as separateness exists only in imagination.

Soul undergoes experience through innumerable forms such as being king and beggar, rich and poor, tall and short, strong and weak, beautiful and ugly, of killing and being killed. All these experiences must transpire as long as the soul, though it is one in reality and undivided, imagines separateness in itself. When soul is bereft of the impressions of these illusionary experiences it becomes naked as in its origin, to become now fully conscious of its unity with the Oversoul which is One, indivisible, Real and Infinite.

The soul becomes free of the binding of impressions through various paths. And love is the most important of these paths leading to the realization of God. Through this love, the soul becomes entirely absorbed in God, ultimately forgetting itself completely. It is then that all of a sudden Knowledge comes as swiftly as the lightning bolt which burns to ashes all that it falls upon.

This Knowledge uproots illusions, doubts and worries, and apparent sufferings are instantaneously replaced by everlasting peace and eternal bliss which is the Goal of all existence. Soul, now free from its illusions, realizes its original unity of being.

* Baba stepped out of the "New Life" in October, 1950 to dictate this message.

Let us not hope, because this Knowledge is beyond hoping and wanting. Let us not reason, because this Knowledge cannot be comprehended or thought of. Let us not doubt, because this Knowledge is the certainty of certainties. Let us not live the life of the senses, because the lusty, greedy, false, impure mind cannot reach this Knowledge. Let us love God as the Soul of our souls and in the height of this love lies this Knowledge.

The divinely Perfect Ones can bestow this Knowledge on any one they like and whenever they like.

May we all gain this Knowledge soon.

My Dear Children

Your coming to me from different places and from across oceans* has pleased me. And although no sacrifice to be near me is too great, I am touched by the sacrifice that some of you have made to come here.

Those who have not been able to come to me should not feel disheartened, for my love is with them as always, and especially so at this time. I know how they are longing to be near me even for an hour, and how helpless they are in their circumstances.

You have come from great distances, not for some convention or conference, but to enjoy my company and feel afresh my love in your hearts. It is a coming together of children of East and West in the house of their Father.

All religions of the world proclaim that there is but one God, the Father of all in creation.

I am that Father.

I have come to remind all people that they should live on earth as the children of the one Father until my grace awakens them to the realization that they are all one without a second, and that all divisions and conflict and hatred are but a shadow-play of their own ignorance.

Although all are my children, they ignore the simplicity and beauty of this Truth by indulging in hatreds, conflicts and wars that divide them in enmity, instead of living as one family in their Father's house. Even amongst you who love me and accept me for what I am, there is sometimes lack of understanding of one another's hearts.

* for a Sahavas of 10,000 lovers at Poona, October, 1962

Patiently have I suffered these things in silence for all my children. It is time that they become aware of the presence of their Father in their midst and of their responsibility towards Him and themselves. I shall break my Silence, and, with my Word of words, arouse my children to realize in their lives, the indivisible Existence which is GOD.

Throughout the years I have been giving many messages and discourses. Today I simply want to tell you who are gathered here in my Love to shut the ears of your minds and open the ears of your hearts to hear my Word when I utter it.

Do not seek my blessing, which is always with you, but long for the day when my grace will descend on all who love me. Most blessed are they who do not even long for my grace, but simply seek to do my will.

My Dear Workers

In spite of telling you very often that I will not give you any more messages or discourses, I find myself doing just this thing which is what I do not want to do. This is because most of you do things which I do not like your doing.

I had to give you a message yesterday because you expected one; and the theme of the message was on your being my children, because despite much talk about a Baba-family, there is more a semblance than a reality of kinship among you who are the children of One Father.

True children of One Father do not greet one another with smiles and embraces and at the same time harbor grudges and ill-feeling, but they have an active concern in their hearts for the well-being of one another and make sacrifices for that well-being.

If you make me your real Father, all differences and contentions between you, and all personal problems in connection with your lives, will become dissolved in the Ocean of my love.

You are all keen on spreading my message of Love and Truth and many of you in the east and west have labored hard in this work; publishing magazines and other literature, organizing meetings, sacrificing your vacations in traveling, building halls and having statues made of me. But I wonder how much of my Love and Truth has been in your work of spreading my message of Love and Truth!

Unless there is a brotherly feeling in your hearts, all the words that you speak or print in my name are hollow; all the miles that you travel in my cause are zero; all organizations for my work are but an appearance of activity; all buildings to contain me are empty places and all statues that you make to embody me are of someone else.

I have been patient and indulgent over the way you have been doing these things, because you have been very young children in my love, and children must have some sort of games to play. But now you are older and are beginning to realize that there is a greater work ahead of you than what you have been doing. And you have been searching your minds and hearts as to what this work might be.

It is not a different work to what you have been already doing . . . it is the same work done in a different way. And that way is the way of effacement, which means the more you work for me the less important you feel in yourself. You must always remember that I alone do my work. Although only the one who has become One with God can serve and work for all, I allow you to work for me so that you have the opportunity to use your talents and capacities selflessly and so draw closer to me. You should never think that in your work for me you are benefiting others, for by being instrumental in bringing others to me you are benefiting yourself.

My work is your opportunity. But when you allow yourself to intervene between you and my work, you are allowing the work to take you away from me. When you put my work before yourself, the work will go right, although not necessarily smoothly. And when the work does not go right, it means you have put yourself between it and its accomplishment.

The way of my work is the way of effacement, which is the way of strength, not of weakness; and through it you become mature in my Love. At this stage you cannot know what real Love is, but through working for me as

you should work for me, you will arrive at that ripeness
where, in a moment, I can give you That which you have
been seeking for millions of years.

The Spiritual Potential of the Film World

For better or for worse, the world of motion pictures has
grown up extensively within the larger world of so-called
realities. But the film world is not foreign to the "real"
world—the two are affiliated so intimately that they can
be seen, essentially, to be made of the same fabric. For
everyone is, in a sense, an actor and the world has often
been compared to the stage by poets and philosophers.
In point of fact, much of what goes for "action" in mod-
ern life can be called little but "acting"; and so the larger
world has little ground to regard only the film world as
being imitative. In the film world, the actor has to think,
feel and act according to the pattern held before him; to
mirror, though temporarily, the personality of the
character being portrayed by him.

This can be said to be equally true, to a considerable
extent, of those outside the world of motion-pictures;
who struggle to follow the conventional pattern of living
as they imagine it is expected of them, even if it cramps
their inner individual expression. This is so not only
figuratively but literally. While looking in the mirror,
people often see themselves more through the eyes of
others than through their own. The reflected image
evokes in their minds the impression they will make on
others and the expectations which others have of
them—and the best that most can do is to try to look the
part they play. Thus the mirror, literally and figuratively,
has become such a seemingly indispensable part of mod-
ern life that we might almost name this age a mirror-
civilization.

When the actor plays the part of a king he knows it to
be an illusion and has, in a sense, an advantage over the
king in the outer world who is not necessarily aware of
any illusion. Both, however, are equally helpless in their
failure to find the Real. No one condemns the actor who
plays the part of an emperor or reformer as a hypocrite,
for although he appears to be what he is not, his honesty
is taken for granted because his audience knows that he is

acting a part. But there are many outside the world of stage and screen who, in actual life, do not appear as they really are. The former are *on* the screen of their creation, the latter *behind* the screen of their creation.

There are specific claims and privileges as well as specific duties and potentialities that no actor can afford to ignore. An actor who may be technically faultless in his part, is yet trivial and worthless if he tries to evade his inherent spiritual potential. The film world cannot escape its obligations to the larger world on which it makes so substantial an impression; and these obligations demand that its spiritual potential take precedence over the desire to make money. The script writers, the producers and the actors should realize their spiritual potential instead of looking at their art as merely or mainly a business. The more vividly they realize this, the more dignified and satisfactory will the result of their efforts be; and their inner account with themselves will be vastly gratifying, even though the same might not be said of their account in the bank. If the film world cannot or will not give the greatest importance to this spiritual potential, it is a failure.

The ordinary man, whose urgent need is to relax from the stress of life, to lessen the sense of insecurity and try to fill the emptiness within (for which greed and war are mostly responsible), turns instinctively to the fleeting diversion of entertainment—and the film world affords this to a great extent. The film world therefore, which still has one of the greatest scopes for influencing the lives of myriads, should ask itself whether it is utilizing its spiritual potential to the full so that man may be helped in his search for Truth, or merely pandering to his pleasure in the false; whether it is encouraging and inspiring youth to face the responsibilities of the world of tomorrow, or retarding youth's inner growth with an overdose of sex and crime films; and whether it is striving after wealth and fame at the cost of man's inherent thirst for the spiritual and uplifting.

The correct solution of every problem can come only from Indivisible Truth. There can be no fictitious cleavage in the unity of life by magnifying the often fallacious distinctions between theory and practice, the artificial and the natural, the real and the false. The emphasis of every aspect of the One Indivisible Life must be on the underlying unity, and not on apparent differences—and this applies with as much force to those in the film world as to those in the outer world.

The great initiator of the Truth of your being is Divine Love—Love that burns the limiting self, that disarms all fears, that rises above temptations, that is deaf to the voices of lust and jealousy, that expresses the infinite spiritual potential. Those in the film world have also to play their part unreservedly in the divine game of life, aspiring to the highest within them; then only can they find real beauty, and then only can they fully express it.

The spiritual potential of those in the film world, though in no way different from that of those outside it, must often be differently expressed. You can, even as an actor, experience and express divinity. In the world of the motion picture and by its means you can learn and you can teach. But if you do not find love or happiness, truth or fulfilment in yourself, you cannot truly impart them to your audience. You cannot inspire, unless you are yourself inspired; nor can you awaken love in insensitive souls without yourself being pierced by it.

The actor has to realize that real and living beauty is made manifest only by discovering and releasing the spiritual potential within himself. Artifice can, no doubt, do much to heighten the fresh and radiant beauty that is natural to youth. But this is artifice, and not art, and such transient beauty is poles apart from real beauty. Without vision your art will be shallow; do not therefore hesitate to glean that vision from the Great Ones. This will give you a living inspiration, bringing fulfilment in your life.

So my message to the film world is: Do not play to the gallery or the salary, but play also to the Infinite within. Live in the presence of God, even while acting your part, so that you can be true to yourself, to your partners and employers, and to the larger and one Indivisible Life of which you are each an inseparable part. *If the world is a stage, God is the only producer, and you can never be anything but a trivial actor if you are not in unison with Him.*

Song of the New Life

Listen to the silent words of Meher Baba;
The life of all lovers of God is in these words.
You who are serious about following the New Life
Will renounce your ephemeral existence.

We have taken to this life in which we rely only upon
God;
Our will is strengthened by our oath.
We merrily sing the song of hopelessness;
We invite all calamities and difficulties.

We neither wail over lost hopes, nor complain about
promises,
Nor covet honour, nor shun disgrace.
Back-biting is ended and we do not fear anyone;
This is the tenor of our New Life.

No confusion in the mind now, neither are any ties left;
Pride, anger, lust and greed are sloughed off.
No religion for any of us, nor care for physical and mental
aims.
The sheik and the Brahmin are now in the same boat.

There is for us all no small or great.
Neither disciple, master, nor Godhood exist.
Brotherliness is the link,
And our common enjoyment of suffering.

This world or the next, hell or heaven, we are no longer
concerned with.
*Shaktis** and *siddhis,** occultism and miracles, we are no
longer plagued with.
All false impressions have been purged from the mind;
Now we live in the active present.

Dear ones, take seriously the words of Baba:
"Although now I am on the same level with you,
Yet all orders from me, good, bad, or extraordinary,
You should carry out immediately, leaving the result to
God.

"Even if the heavens fall,
Do not let go the hand of Truth;

* occult powers

Let not despair or disappointment ravage and destroy the
    garden of your life;
You beautify it by contentment and self-sufficiency.

"Even though your heart be cut to bits, let a smile be on
    your lips.
Here I divulge to you a truth:
Hidden in your empty hands is treasure untold;
Your beggarly life is the envy of kings.

"God exists indeed, and true are the Prophets,
Every cycle has an *Avatar,* and every moment a *wali.*†
For us, however, it is only hopelessness and helplessness,
How else can I describe to you what our New Life is?"

A Prayer For Baba's Lovers
Dictated by Meher Baba

Beloved God, help us all to love You more and
more,
    And more and more and still yet more,
    Till we become worthy of union with You;
    And help us all to hold fast to Baba's *Daaman* till the
very end.

† saint